TITO

I0873707

Stevan K. Pavlowitch

TITO

Yugoslavia's Great Dictator

A Reassessment

OHIO STATE UNIVERSITY PRESS
COLUMBUS

First published in the United States of America
by Ohio State University Press
Published simultaneously in the United Kingdom
by C. Hurst & Co. (Publishers) Ltd.

Library of Congress Cataloging-in-Publication Data

Pavlowitch, Stevan K.
  Tito — Yugoslavia's great dictator : a reassassment / Stevan K.
Pavlowitch
     p. cm.
  Includes bibliographical references and index.
  ISBN 0-8142-0600-X
  1. Tito, Josip Broz, 1892–1980. 2. Presidents — Yugoslavia —
Biography. 3. Communists — Yugoslavia — Biography. 4. Yugoslavia —
History — 1945–1980. I. Title.
DR1300.P38 1992
949.702'3'092 — dc20
  [B]   92-23760
                                                                 CIP

Printed in Hong Kong

The paper in this book meets the guidelines for permanence and
durability of the Committee on Production Guidelines for Book
Longevity of the Council on Library Resources. ∞

9 8 7 6 5 4 3 2 1

CONTENTS

PREFACE

Now that the collapse of Communism and the break-up of Yugoslavia call into question the purposes to which Tito's energies were devoted, the outside world has largely forgotten that it praised him for being one of the giants of our time, the great commander, revolutionary, heretic and statesman who stood up to Hitler and Stalin, who unified his compatriots in war and peace on the bases of brotherhood, self-management socialism and non-alignment, and who appealed, in one way or another, at one time or another, to West, East and Third World, to Right, Left and Centre. In Yugoslavia, adoration has given way to amnesia and demonisation.

It is surely worth reminding those who adored him, those who praised him, those who hated him, and those who have forgotten him, that their attitudes give us ample justification for considering Tito to have indeed been, in his own way, one of the 'great men' of our century, and that the time has come to try and suggest a more analytical approach to the man who reigned over Yugoslavia for thirty-five years.

It is the historian's task not to pass moral judgement, but rather to try and make the past more intelligible and, in the case of a leader like Tito, to try and link his rôle to the events that came after him.

In order to do that, I have read again all the books of any substance (as well as many of the writings of no substance) that were devoted to him and his achievements during his lifetime. I have also read most of what has been published about him since his death (including much of the trash). I have not gone into the archives, even though there is much material relating to Tito lying in diplomatic, military, security and Party archives in Belgrade, and in his own papers now collected in the Josip Broz Tito Memorial Centre. Some of it is available; most of it is still inaccessible.

Memoirs have shed new light on personalities, atmosphere and details, but the hard evidence for the motives of decision-makers has not yet appeared. Sensational claims have been made, with little back-up beyond prejudice, wishful thinking or, at best, plausibility. Wild rumours circulated about Tito's true identity during the war, and Evelyn Waugh is known to have maliciously reported that he was perhaps a woman, but rumours keep circulating. Was Josip Broz the illegitimate son of a count? Was he, perhaps, a Hungarian Jew? Was he not a Freemason? Did he have a secret meeting with Pope Pius XII in August 1944? Did the real Josip Broz die in the Spanish civil war, or even at the beginning of the partisan struggle in Yugoslavia? Are the remains of Marshal Tito really buried in his mausoleum? More seriously, we really know very little of Tito's early life and of his relations with his family. There are still many missing pieces of the jigsaw, which makes it difficult, for instance, to get a fuller picture of his work for the Comintern, in Moscow and in Paris, or of the dissensions that remained in the leadership of the Communist Party of Yugoslavia on the eve of the Second World War.

Then, during the war, Tito was keen to play down the extent of the civil war, and to portray himself, to the Western Allies, but also to the Yugoslavs, as a national unifier first and foremost — a view that was greatly reinforced when he successfully stood up to Stalin only a few years after the end of the war. A whole school of interpretation then sought to show how he had always put Yugoslavia's national interests above those of international Communism.

When de-Titoisation took off, silently and discreetly, the memoirs of his lieutenants, ministers, generals and ambassadors revealed numerous contradictions. He seemed to have been both a ruthless revolutionary and an imaginative statesman, both a successfully dogmatic hard-liner and a triumphant heretic *malgré lui*, a good disciple of Soviet Stalinism and a manipulator of some sort of a Yugoslav Marxism. He often pursued contradictory policies, and was not afraid of appearing to 'switch track' in order to 'keep on the rails'.

Any critical approach to Tito was taboo for several years after his death. At the end of the 1980s in Yugoslavia, as a reaction to almost half a century of personality cult, the hero was turned into a villain. Myths crumbled, and Tito was blamed for everything. Of the two major national groups, Serbs perceived him as having divided them in order to satisfy all the other nationalities, and the Croats as having curtailed their national re-awakening in order to satisfy the Serbs. The general public was avid for descriptions of his life of luxury and lust. Only Djilas attempted to do justice to him while demolishing many of his claims to greatness.

While trying to explain that the seeds of his long-term failure lay in his short-term successes, and that the style and substance of his régime provided little more than transient unity, I admit that Tito still remains something of a mystery to me. It may be that all we can see to date is but an appearance, the mask of a ruler, since the important mechanisms of his régime always functioned behind close doors. Or it may even be that there was little more to the régime than an epic-looking décor, and nothing more to him than a manipulator of genius. Could he have been a 'wonderful Wizard of Oz'?[1] After having distilled three years of research, thinking and writing into these hundred pages, I still do not have the answer.

There has been no anti-Communist revolution in Yugoslavia. The régime has merely disintegrated. And it has disintegrated into a sordid and tragic game of post-Communist republican *nomenklaturas* turned into ethnarchies, who have moved from totalitarian Communism, issuing calls for class struggle under the guise of internationalism, to totalitarian nationalism, whipping up ethnic struggle and masquerading as democracy. Europe probably misunderstands Tito's heirs as much as it misunderstood Tito himself.

This study has had quite a few readers already; I thank them all for their suggestions, even when these were not taken up, and for pointing out a number of errors. My acknowledgements are in particular due to a few critical and rational friends, colleagues

---

[1] 'I have fooled everyone so long that I thought I should never be found out' (L.F. Baum, *The Wonderful Wizard of Oz*, ch. XV). Professor Žarko Puhovksi made the Wizard of Oz a symbol of Communism in general at the founding conference of the Centre for the Study of the Transformation of Central and Eastern Europe, held at the London School of Economics on 25 January 1992.

and acquaintances in both Belgrade and Zagreb who read, or with whom I discussed, parts of the manuscript; to Mr A.S. Burn, who has again drawn the maps as in my previous books; to Mrs Vera Gajić who loaned us the gold coin reproduced on the book's cover and Mr Paul Fox who photographed it; and to the Committee of Advanced Studies of the University of Southampton, who provided funds to release me from teaching duties one summer term.

At the very end, I wish to thank Anne and Noël Rey, who put me up and put up with me while I was polishing this attempted reassessment of the Great Dictator who was deemed by some enthusiasts, at the end of the Second World War, to be the one who would 'bring freedom, democracy and social justice' to all the peoples of the Balkans; whom the most lucid of French political thinkers thought, a few years later at the time of the 'break with Stalin', to be but the most glorious of the 'red kinglets of the Balkans'; to whom one of his most persistent British admirers was still grateful, after he had inaugurated the last, rather depressive decade of his reign, for being one of the 'few uncommon men who are still left to us'; whom the US Secretary of State still described diplomatically, but probably sincerely, two years after his death, as a 'great leader and world statesman'; and of whom some of my students had no longer even heard by 1989.

This book is for all those who, like me, are trying to understand Tito and what people made of him. It is also for all students of Yugoslavia, of the Yugoslav lands, kingdoms, principalities, republics, provinces, cantons, territories, fiefs, nations, nationalities, tribes, majorities and minorities which are gradually forgetting him. It is dedicated to the memory of my Mother, who did not really try to understand him, and did not like him either.

Marnes-la-Coquette   ST.K. PAVLOWITCH
January 1992

CHRONOLOGY

1892 Josip Broz (later known as Tito) born at Kumrovec, 7 May

1907 Goes to work in industry

1913 Joins Austro-Hungarian army

1915 Captured in Russia

1918 Unified Kingdom of the Serbs, Croats and Slovenes proclaimed, 1 December

1920 Tito returns home from Russia

1927 Becomes secretary to Zagreb KPJ Committee

1929 Begins to serve prison sentence; King Alexander abolishes parliamentary government; name of country officially changed to Yugoslavia

1934 Tito released from prison; King Alexander assassinated

1935 Tito sent to work for Comintern in Moscow

1937 Called to Paris to head caretaker KPJ leadership

1940 Confirmed as secretary Central Committee KPJ

1941 Axis powers invade Yugoslavia, April; collapse, occupation, partition and civil war follow; Tito calls population to aid Soviet Union, July; leaves Belgrade to join partisans, September

1943 Negotiates with German command, March; holds Jajce congress to lay foundations of future Communist régime, November

1944 Returns to liberated Belgrade, October

1945 President of Provisional Government, March

1948 KPJ expelled from Cominform

1953 Tito formally head of state

1955 Bulganin and Khrushchev visit Belgrade, reconciliation with Soviet Union formalised

1956 Relations strained again after Hungarian revolution crushed

1961 Belgrade Conference of Non-Aligned States

1963 No limitation of mandate for Tito under new Constitution

1968 Tito condemns Soviet intervention in Czechoslovakia, and faces students' revolt and other mass demonstrations

1971 Initiates 'counter-reform', purges and 'feudalises' Party apparatus

1974 Another Constitution fixes new concept of eight-unit quasi-confederation under Tito's life presidency

1978 Tito implements collective leadership

1979 Last pilgrimage to Moscow

1980 Dies in Ljubljana, 4 May

ABBREVIATIONS

The following upper-case abbreviations have been used, derived from Serbo-Croatian names of institutions:

AVNOJ   Anti-Fascist Council for the National Liberation of Yugoslavia, the 'parliament' of the Communist-led People's Liberation Movement during the Second World War

KPJ   Communist Party of Yugoslavia, later known as SKJ, League of Communists of Yugoslavia

NDH   Independent State of Croatia, the greater Croatian state set up by the Ustaša movement under the aegis of Germany and Italy during the Second World War

NOV   People's Liberation Army, the official name of the Communist-led partisans during the Second World War

SKJ   League of Communists of Yugoslavia (see above under KPJ)

MAPS

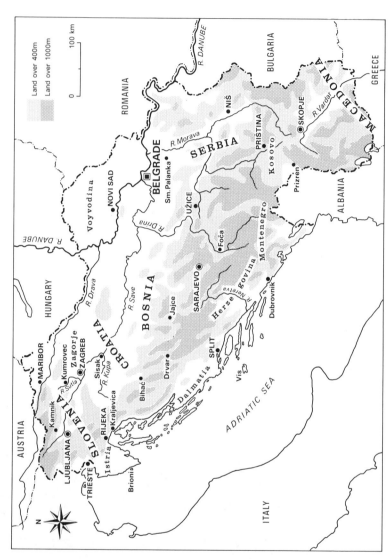

Yugoslavia

The Yugoslav lands on the eve of the First World War.

The federated units of Yugoslavia after the Second World War.

'I believe that not only the Yugoslavs but all the Balkan peoples will one day revere Tito as the great man in whose achievements their aspirations also had a stake [. . .] The new Yugoslavia brings freedom, democracy and social justice not only to Yugoslavs. The turning point in the history of the Balkans has been reached. Just as the new Yugoslavia can only be Tito's Yugoslavia, so the new Balkans can only be Tito's Balkans.' (Michael Padev, *Marshal Tito*, London, 1944)

'De tous les roitelets rouges des Balkans, Tito était le plus glorieux.' (Raymond Aron, 10 July 1948, in *Les Articles du Figaro*, I, ed. by Georges-Marie Soutou, Paris, 1990)

'When the Century of the Common Man approaches its last quarter, one cannot help feeling grateful for a few uncommon men who are still left to us. Tito, whatever view you take of him, is certainly one of these.' (Fitzroy Maclean, in *The Sunday Times*, 3 May 1970)

'The great leader and world statesman who has led the Yugoslav peoples out of the ruins of the war, to stability at home, to respect and prestige in the world.' (Alexander Haig, US Secretary of State, in the visitors' book at Tito's tomb, as quoted in *Politika*, Belgrade, 4 May 1982)

'Tito? Who's he?' (second-year history student at Southampton University, starting a Balkan History course, 5 October 1989)

'Tito is ours! Tito is yours! Tito was ours, and you were Tito's, but that's not my fault. . . .' (parody of the old propaganda song 'Tito is ours, we are Tito's', popularised by the Belgrade rock-singer Bora Djordjević, known as Bora Čorba)

1

THE EARLY YEARS, 1892–1920:
GASTARBEITER AND N.C.O.

Childhood

Marshal Tito, ruler of Communist Yugoslavia from the end of the Second World War to his death in 1980, as secretary-general of the Party, head of government, commander-in-chief and then life president, was born Josip Broz on 7 May 1892,[1] in the village of Kumrovec, in the region of Croatia known as Zagorje, some 50 kilometres north-west of Zagreb, in what was then Austria-Hungary.

The crown of Croatia had been united with that of Hungary since 1102 — a date that marks the beginning of Croatia's eight-centuries-long association with, and domination by, Hungary. In 1526–7, when a large part of its territory had been conquered by the Ottoman Turks, the Habsburgs were elected to what remained of the Hungaro-Croatian realm before proceeding to reconquer in their entirety the 'dominions of the Crown of Hungary' in the seventeenth and eighteenth centuries, and going on to acquire more South Slav populations. They already had the Slovenes in the southern part of their Austrian hereditary lands. Through the Hungarian connexion, they would rule Croatia. They were going to acquire the once Venetian Adriatic province of Dalmatia after the fall of Napoleon, in 1815, and the Turkish provinces of Bosnia and Herzegovina at the Congress of Berlin, in 1878.

In 1867 — twenty-five years before Josip Broz was born — the old family conglomerate ruled over by the House of Habsburg became the Dual Monarchy, or Austria-Hungary. It was

---

[1] His birthday was officially celebrated on 25 May as the Day of Youth. The date had been fixed during the war, before Tito's appointed biographer, Vladimir Dedijer, had been able to get his researchers to check the parish registers. Tito himself was not quite sure.

1

reorganised on the basis of a 'compromise' which satisfied the Hungarians, or at any rate the Hungarian gentry, at the expense of the other, smaller nationalities. The dynastic lands were turned into two constitutional states with a common monarch — Emperor of Austria and King of Hungary — and some other joint institutions. These arrangements were complemented the following year by a second compromise, a sort of sub-compromise within historic Hungary, whereby Croatia (officially called the Kingdom of Croatia-Slavonia) was accorded a special status as an 'adjacent territory' of the Hungarian crown, and a certain amount of autonomy in running its administration, judiciary and education. It thereafter had a local legislature, called the *Sabor*, and a local executive under a Hungarian-appointed governor, or *ban*.

In the reorganised Dual Monarchy, the South Slavs were as divided as ever. The smaller group of Slovenes — about 1.1 million — were scattered through six Austrian provinces ruled from Vienna. Dalmatia, with a population of under half a million, mostly Croats but with 16 per cent Serbs, was also an Austrian province. In the Hungarian half of the monarchy, ruled from Budapest, about 14 per cent of the population were made up of Croats and Serbs, some 1.9 million of them (including half a million Serbs) in Croatia. More South Slavs — 1.2 million Orthodox (Serbs), Muslims and Catholics (Croats) — were acquired when Austria-Hungary took over the administration of Bosnia-Herzegovina, which was formally annexed as a joint possession of Austria and Hungary in 1908.

Tito was the seventh of fifteen children born to Franjo and Marija Broz (a short form of Ambroz — Ambrose), seven of whom survived to become adults. Kumrovec, his birth-place, lies in the valley of the river Sutla, which divides Croatia from Slovenia, two parts of the then Dual Monarchy, the one Hungarian and the other Austrian, but also two distinct, if related, South Slav linguistic areas. It boasts two tourist attractions: the more recent, much restored and museified family home of its most famous son, and the more ancient, abandoned and ruined castle of its one-time Hungarian lords, the Erdödy family, who had been there since the early sixteenth century, but sold out and left after the abolition of serfdom in 1848.

The Broz house — four rooms, hall and kitchen, shared with a cousin — is among the best in the village, even making allowances for its restoration. Franjo Broz owned 15 acres of land, but financial irresponsibility had led him to fall into debt and take to drink. Even though he lived on to the age of eighty, the family burden fell early upon his wife, the eldest of fourteen children of a better-off Slovenian peasant across the river. This grandfather took the three-year-old Josip to live with him until he was of school age, when he returned to attend elementary school in his native village and to work on his father's farm.

Economic difficulties were forcing the pace of change in rural Croatia. Serfdom had been abolished, even though that had been little more than the legal acknowledgement of an accomplished fact. The peasants had become the owners of the plots they tilled, but the gentry received compensation, and kept the remaining lands. This enabled large estates and the power of the landed nobility — largely alien in the case of the non-Magyar regions of Hungary — to survive until the First World War. Quite apart from there not being enough land to go around for the peasants, Hungary as a whole experienced an agrarian crisis, compounded by a series of bad harvests between 1870 and 1890, due to the competition of cheaper imports of foreign, essentially American, grain.

Government subsidies, protective tariffs, and support for the introduction of more modern farming methods benefited the large estate-owners but not the smallholders, who had difficulty in surviving. Still paying off the acquisition of their holdings, they suffered from higher food prices when a bad harvest meant that they did not have enough grain for the whole year, and they suffered from lower food prices when a good year meant that the price for their surplus was forced down. Becoming landless labourers or emigrating was often the only answer to their problems.

From around 1880, the Hungarian part of the monarchy experienced a wave of emigration, with the minorities over-represented among the emigrants. Most went overseas, but others simply to the more developed and industrialised Austrian lands, and from countryside to towns: the same period saw rapid growth of industry, commerce and transport in Austria-Hungary. Even Croatia was industrialised from the late 1890s, with a corresponding increase in the number of factory-workers. Industrial labour being still often seasonal, many workers spent part of the year on the land as peasants. The drift of young peasants to towns was part of the process of disintegration of patriarchal society — the result of paucity of land, a growing population and rising food prices. Between 190,000 and 250,000 people emigrated from Croatia to America in the period 1890–1913, and many went off to work in the towns, in Austria and in Germany.

Martin Broz, an older brother, had already left home while Tito was still at school. He would eventually settle in Hungary and remain there until his death, after the Second World War. Like Stalin's mother, Tito's mother, who was religious, wanted her Josip to become a priest, but he dreamed of better-dressed callings, such as being a waiter or a policeman. The family had a relation who was a sergeant in Sisak, a garrison town and road junction south-east of Zagreb. When the military cousin once came home to Kumrovec, he told Tito that he knew of a retired sergeant in Sisak who had a regimental canteen and was in need of a young waiter. Franjo Broz had thought of sending Josip to America, but the trip was beyond his means, so in 1907, at the age of fifteen, Tito went off to Sisak.

Locksmith's apprentice and assistant

Tito's peasant childhood had come to an end, and he was about to become what would be known in Yugoslavia, in the later years of his rule, as a *gastarbeiter*, an emigrant 'guest'-worker. His aim from now on was to get on in life. His first ambition was to go off to town, and earn enough to eat well and dress smartly. At one time a stronghold against the Turks, where the river Kupa flows into the Save, Sisak in 1907 was a town of 7,500 inhabitants at the end of a branch of the Vienna-Trieste railway. Tito started work as a Jack-of-all-trades in the canteen next to the barracks of the 77th Territorial Regiment. He found it an agreeable place, frequented by officers and non-commissioned officers, with an orchestra in the evening, but he was made to work too hard for his liking, and therefore soon moved on to something better through his acquaintance with locksmith apprentices.

He had himself formally apprenticed to a locksmith, who was in fact the owner of a mechanical workshop. A locksmith was also a general mechanic, and considered a specialised craftsman. By the contract signed with Tito's father, the owner provided training and keep for three years. This was one of the larger mechanical workshops in Croatia at the time, with a couple of assistants and three or four apprentices. As one of these, Josip Broz had become part of the 8.6 per cent of the population of Croatia employed in industry, crafts and transport. Apprentices had to attend evening classes twice each week at a technical school, and Tito later recalled these years with pleasure. He liked his boss and his teachers, and told his biographers that he read all he could lay his hands on. He was full of admiration for town life — the uniforms, the officers, and the cafés with their music, singing and pornographic films.

Tito's Sisak years — 1907–10 — were an important period in the history of the South Slavs. Initially, under the 1868 constitutional arrangements, Croatia's limited autonomy meant some security before the law for all its inhabitants. It also meant that the Budapest government's Magyarisation measures were not implemented there to the same degree as elsewhere, where only one indivisible Hungarian 'political nation' was acknowledged within the borders of historic Hungary. However, when Count Kuehn-Héderváry was governor, in the twenty-year period 1883–1903, not only did the policy of Magyarisation intensify, but the Hungarian government also began to exploit the rivalries between Croats and Serbs within the context of Croatia's autonomy, in order to play off the two communities against each other.

After 1903, the dynastic change in Serbia signalled the advent there of a parliamentary democratic government under King Peter I and the popular Radical Party. This coincided with a new internal crisis between Vienna and Budapest, and both series of events accelerated the development of the South Slav, or Yugoslav, movement. Ever since 1804, when the Serbs of the province of Belgrade had risen against the Sultan's rebellious Janissary troops, an autonomous principality of Serbia had grown to the point of becoming a fully independent state in 1878, and a kingdom in 1882. Intellectuals and politicians, in both Zagreb and Belgrade, had intermittently been in touch with each other, and kept the mystique of South Slav unity as an ultimate aim. The ideal of a wide Yugoslav community, based on similarities of popular speech and culture, had been spreading since the 1830s among the younger urban intelligentsia. It was the basis for Austria-Hungary's distrust of independent Serbia, which lay outside the control of the Habsburg Monarchy.

In Croatia, faced with the intransigent attitude of the author-ities, part of a new generation was beginning to break with legalism. Serbs were turning against concessions designed to pro-mote Hungarian interests. The young in both communities were coming together to demand social reforms and the democratisa-tion of political life. At the time, only some 45,000 out of a total population of 2,416,000 were entitled to vote. A small, tolerated trade union movement had been created in the 1890s, and though not yet interested in broader social or political issues, it was achiev-ing some success in immediate down-to-earth questions such as wages. A Social-Democratic Party of Croatia-Slavonia had also been established. It was politically moderate, supporting the estab-lished parties of the electorate in the struggle to obtain more autonomy for Croatia. It was also demanding universal suffrage to implement social and economic reforms.

There was considerable improvement in the political climate of Croatia after 1903. Croatian opposition deputies came together with the political representatives of the Serbs in the province to form a Croato-Serbian Coalition, which won the 1906 elections to the Sabor. Trade unions were legalised. Croatian discontent with Budapest turned to solidarity with the Serbs — not only those of Austria-Hungary but also those of independent Serbia. A new Croatian Peasant Party came into being, with the aim of bringing the peasant masses to politics, and of carrying out an agrarian reform.

Socialist-led agitation among the industrial workers did lead to the working day being limited to nine or eight hours, and socialist propaganda even managed to stimulate some response in the countryside, notably in Zagorje, where the demand for a general franchise and for social reform could appeal to the impoverished peasantry. Although by 1906 there were already some 13,000 industrial workers and 2,500 agricultural labourers organised by the Social-Democratic Party, its influence was still limited to a small section of the working class. Before 1914, there was just one Social-Democratic representative in the Sabor, along with three from the Croatian Peasant Party. Apathy more than oppression was the main enemy.

There is no evidence that in Kumrovec, where there were only three voters, either the Social-Democratic or the Croatian Peasant Party had any influence on the Broz family. Politically, Sisak was one of the centres of the Croato-Serbian coalition, but although Tito said much later that he sympathised with the Social Democrats, it was only towards the very end of his stay in that town that the party organised itself there, with some fifty workers affiliated to a union. In the autumn of 1910, having obtained his certificate as a locksmith's assistant, Tito left for Zagreb in search of better employment. There, in the capital of the realm of Croatia-Slavonia, a city of 75,000 inhabitants, he obtained work at a locksmith's again, and registered with the Metal Workers' Union. This also made him automatically a member of the Social-Democratic Party.

In the last few years of the Habsburg Monarchy, those among the South Slav socialists who favoured the creation of some sort of a Yugoslavia were called 'nationalists' by the proponents of reform within Austria-Hungary. The latter, who described themselves as 'internationalists', were moderates in comparison to the former, who manifested greater dissatisfaction with the social conditions and the conditions of the nationalities in the Dual Monarchy. The 'nationalists' believed that these could only be altered by revolution, and advocated a radical transformation of both the social and the international order, but they represented no more than a fringe of the workers of Croatia until well into the First World War.

The 'internationalists', on the other hand, were achieving

results in their efforts to improve working conditions. They were firmly rooted in the trade union movement of the Monarchy, and strongly represented in the socialist movement of Croatia. They too believed in some form of Yugoslav unity, but they feared upheavals that could lead to the destruction of Austria-Hungary — a state that had a powerful Social-Democratic movement which was achieving considerable successes in improving the standard of living of the working class.

From 1912 on, the situation deteriorated rapidly throughout the South Slav areas of Austria-Hungary. Serbia's successes in all fields — political, cultural, economic and, in the Balkan Wars, military — caused pro-Serbian demonstrations and strikes in Croatia which led to a renewed suspension of constitutional arrangements by the Hungarian government. Serbia once again became the focus of many hopes. Rejecting legal action for piecemeal reforms and fractional unification within the Monarchy, more and more of the young turned to violent action for a united, complete and independent state of Yugoslavia. That generation of Croatian, Serbian and Slovenian students in Austria-Hungary was the first to think in terms of a break-up of the centuries-old dynastic state. Revolutionary ferment was spreading throughout the Yugoslav territories of the Habsburgs. There was a growing feeling of South Slav solidarity. Yet, on the whole, in 1914, openly anti-Habsburg aspirations were still limited to a fringe, and the vast majority of Croatia's predominantly rural population remained loyal to the Empire and its dynasty until the end of the First World War.

Gastarbeiter

Tito was not part of that revolutionary Yugoslav ferment. Indeed, in spite of his alleged Social-Democratic sympathies, political activity did not yet play an important part in his life. His main objective seems to have been to go back home with money to show for his success. This he did with the onset of the winter of 1910, after having worked for a couple of months in Zagreb. Back in Kumrovec over the winter with some savings, he helped at home, yet he soon wanted to go off again to find fulfilment as a skilled mechanic. In mid-winter he went to Ljubljana, and thence to Trieste. He travelled with his father's horse-drawn cart to the nearest railway station, and then by train, but eventually on foot. He was unlucky in both cities and, having spent his money, had to walk or hitch-hike back to Kumrovec. The only interesting point in this venture is that in Trieste he was able to claim some help from the local branch of the trade union of which he was still nominally a member. In March, however, he returned to Zagreb, with more luck in so far as he found better employment in a workshop which repaired various machines, including motor-cars. There Tito had his first experience not only of automobiles but also of what is now called industrial action — the May 1911 strike of locksmith workers for a nine-hour day and higher pay, which was in part successful.

As soon as he had earned enough money, he would buy himself a new suit, and then think of going in search of better employment, but also further away from his father, who demanded more and more of his son's money. There were many like him. Real colonies of workers from Croatia were to be found in the industrial centres of Austria-Hungary, and even in Germany, some of them settling for shorter or longer periods, others more nomadic.

From Zagreb, Tito soon went again to Ljubljana and to a metal-goods factory nearby, at Kamnik, employing some 150 workers. There not only was he able to spend more on his appearance, but he actually joined Sokol, the patriotic gymnastic organisation, less — so his sympathetic biographer of the 1960s, Phyllis Auty, tells us — for its covertly anti-Habsburg and pro-Yugoslav ideology than for its smart uniform and proud displays. Whatever his reasons, his membership of Sokol brought him into direct contact with people who believed, and actively so, that Slovenes, Croats and Serbs were but three tribes to be united into one modern nation.

The Kamnik works went bankrupt and closed in May 1912. Tito found himself one of a group of redundant workers who were offered a month's wages in advance to go to a large factory in Bohemia where labour was needed. They went there, and found that they had been recruited as strike-breakers. Nevertheless, they were in one of the more expanding industrial areas of Europe, and did find employment. Tito was now truly out of his linguistic territory (both Croat and Slovene), though still in Slavonic-speaking regions. He picked up some Czech while working there over the summer, eventually in the Škoda works at Plzen (Pilsen). He soon left Austria-Hungary for Germany, journeying from one industrial centre to another, taking a job for a short time, and travelling on — to Munich, to Mannheim, and as far west as the Ruhr, picking up German after Czech. Again the twenty-year-old Tito was not alone in this. He was merely doing what many of his young compatriots were doing at the time — keeping on the move, improving his skills, picking up a smattering of foreign languages, and walking more than he rode on trains.

It was when he was in Mannheim, working for Benz, that for the second time in his life he thought of emigrating to America. But instead of going even further west across the ocean, he actually retraced his steps, working his way back nearer home at the end of 1913. His elder brother Martin was by then settled with a family near Vienna, working as a railwayman at Wiener Neustadt station, and Josip joined him. On the strength of his experience with Benz at Mannheim, he obtained employment at the Daimler factory at Wiener Neustadt. He later boasted that he had even been a test-driver. The Vienna period, like that at Sisak, was one that Tito remembered as one he had enjoyed. He loved strolling and gazing at his betters. Aiming ever higher, taking delight in appearances and in status symbols, he even took fencing and waltzing lessons.

N.C.O. and P.O.W.

Thereafter, less is known of his life until 1920, and the next seven years have to be pieced together mostly on the basis of Tito's own reminiscences — which contain contradictions. In the autumn of 1913, he had to return to Croatia for his military service, which he did with the 25th Croatian Territorial Infantry Regiment, based in Zagreb. Before the year was out, apparently at his own request, he was received into a school for non-commissioned officers. He did well, becoming a good skier and a good fencer, and the youngest corporal and then the youngest sergeant in the regiment. He took part in army fencing championships, and obtained awards, including a period of special leave.

When Austria-Hungary attacked Serbia in July 1914, thus starting the Great War, Sergeant Broz was sent to the Serbian front with the 10th Company, 25th Croatian Territorial Infantry Regiment, 42nd Division. This was long kept a state secret in Communist Yugoslavia. In 1951, Vladimir Dedijer was told not to mention the fact in his official biography, even though the unit and Tito remained on the Drina sector of the Serbian front only until the end of 1914. In January 1915, they were transferred to the Eastern Front, in the Carpathians, in anticipation of the new Russian offensive there.

Later, in the 1950s, Tito would say that, as a soldier, he had viewed Austria-Hungary as an oppressive state, that he and his comrades had looked on the war as offering the subject nationalities a chance to free themselves from Habsburg rule, that he had disliked the war but that he had hoped it would bring about a dissolution of the hated Monarchy. He used to claim that he had spoken out against the Habsburgs, and that his words had been reported, causing him to be put under arrest for a day in Petrovaradin (Peterwardein) fortress. Such reminiscences sound somewhat contrived, and contradict other statements of his, that his brief incarceration in Petrovaradin had been due to a bureaucratic mistake, that he had enjoyed army life and had not been very politically-minded at the time.

On balance, young Tito seems to have been rather a conformist, and to have been considered by his superiors as good material for promotion. He was certainly not the only South Slav soldier of the Habsburg Emperor and King to have fought against Serbia, for the troops sent initially to teach that country a lesson were made up mostly of Yugoslavs from the regiments of Croatia, and even included many Serbs. These were the descendants of the Orthodox farmer-soldiers who had been resettled in the one-time Military Frontier (*Militärgrenze* or *Vojna Krajina* — Krajina for short) of the Monarchy to bolster up its defences against the Turks in the seventeenth and eighteenth centuries, and they were the forefathers of the Serbs in the present-day republic of Croatia. The Emperor's South Slav subjects had played an important part in the wars of those times, when the regiments from Croatia had become a household word all over Europe, often left to pillage in order to frighten people with their 'Turkish' aspect, and incidentally bequeathing to us the use of the cravat.

When the Russian spring offensive began in 1915 in the Carpathians, Tito was put in charge of a reconnoitring section operating behind enemy lines. He did not, like so many of his Slav compatriots in the Austro-Hungarian forces on the Eastern Front, go over to the Russians or even surrender to them. On the contrary, he distinguished himself, fully earning the confidence of his commanders. It was discovered in 1980 that he had actually been recommended for an award for gallantry and initiative in reconnaissance and in capturing prisoners.

Tito was even wounded in action, and it was only when his battalion was surrounded by Circassian cavalry, and he was himself again seriously wounded, that he was taken prisoner in April 1915. Even then, he did not enlist with the Yugoslav prisoners-of-war who were volunteering to join the Serbian army. He first spent a whole year recuperating from his wound, at a monastery turned into a hospital for prisoners-of-war. This is the second period in his life, after Sisak, during which he says that he read — in Russian this time. For all its Slav affinities with the Serbo-Croatian and Slovenian speech native to him, and in spite of his smattering of Czech, Russian was a new language, and one written in another script. Even after he had recovered, he did not want to enrol in the volunteers being trained to be sent to the Dobrudja front in Romania, but chose instead to work as a mechanic in a mill.

In the summer of 1916, along with other Austro-Hungarian prisoners, he was transferred to the foothills of the Urals, at Kungur in the government of Perm, to work on the repair of the railways. There he acted as overseer in a small camp where little was known of what was going on elsewhere in Russia or on the fronts. In fact, it was uncertain to what extent they were still considered to be captives. With the surveillance somewhat relaxed, Tito escaped in June 1917, and made his way to Petrograd (the Russianised name of Saint Petersburg), not to take part in the Revolution, but to find better work in his own speciality.

He later told Milovan Djilas that he thought it was all over with the Revolution. Demonstrations were still going on, however, and he actually toyed once more (the third time) with the idea of emigrating to the United States. He revealed this in one of his television reminiscences, in 1976, when he added half-jokingly: 'Had I done it, I would have become a millionaire!' He went so far as to try and get to Finland; he was caught, returned to Petrograd, and sent back to Kungur, but he gave his guards the slip on the way.

He thus found his way to Siberia, arriving in Omsk some time in the autumn of 1917, when the Bolsheviks were already in power there. Once again, he teamed up with a group of former prisoners-of-war, Austro-Hungarian Slavs and Romanians, working off and on as a mechanic at the railway station. Our knowledge of this period of Tito's life relies mainly on his own account, which is not always very precise.

He moved out to a Kirghiz village some 40 kilometres away, when the White forces of Admiral Kolchak took over in Omsk. This, Dedijer tells us, was to avoid being conscripted into the Czech or Serbian volunteers. While with the Kirghizes, he again worked at a mill. It seems that he joined the Red Guards at some stage, and that in the spring of 1918 he applied for membership of the Communist Party. His Party card would say that he was registered with the Omsk party on 19 January 1919. But at that time Omsk was under the Whites; the Reds did not take over again until August. Anyway, Austria-Hungary was by then already dead and in the process of being buried. On 29 October 1918, the Sabor of Croatia-Slavonia had cut off all its links with Hungary and with the Habsburg dynasty; on 12 November, the Republic of Austria had been proclaimed, on 16 November the Republic of Hungary, and on 1 December the unification of the Kingdom of the Serbs, Croats and Slovenes (Yugoslavia for short, but not yet officially so named). How much did Tito in Omsk know of what was happening, in Russia, in central Europe and in the Balkans? At one stage, in 1945, he admitted frankly that his membership of the Red Guards or Communist Party in 1918–19 hardly counted, as 'it was all very crazy'.

On arriving at Omsk, in November 1917, he had met a local girl, Pelagija Belousova, the daughter of a peasant, and he was married to her there in the summer of 1919. Soon after his marriage, he decided he wanted to go home. Once the railways started moving again with some semblance of regularity, with his Russian wife he took the train to Petrograd. There he joined a group of Yugoslav ex-P.O.W.s who wanted to make their way home, and they set off on a long journey, first to Narva, where they boarded a ship to Stettin. Leaving Stettin in March 1920, they made their way through Germany, and six months later were able to contact the Yugoslav consulate in Vienna. Josip Broz was back in Kumrovec in October 1920, aged twenty-eight, after an absence of six years.

The impression that one gets of Tito during this period is of a young boy desperate to get away from the hard life of his native village. He dreams of appearances: waiters and non-commissioned officers wear smart clothes, and those occupations consequently appeal to him. His aim in life is to learn a craft that will enable him to earn a better living in urban industries. The pattern is set. He works long enough to send money home at first, and to buy himself a suit, before he is off again in search of a better job and to see the world. Military service then opens the prospect of army life, at which he is successful in peace and war, until he is wounded and captured. In spite of what he later told his biographer, and of vague left-wing leanings — towards the Social Democrats in Austria-Hungary and the Bolsheviks in Russia —, there is really no evidence to show that he was ever deeply committed politically before he returned to Yugoslavia. His half-joke about becoming a millionaire had he emigrated to the United States might even indicate that personal ambition led to revolutionary zeal, rather than the other way round.

2

IN AND OUT OF YUGOSLAVIA: 1920–1941: CONSPIRATOR

Trade unionist and Party official

Profound changes had taken place at home since Tito had gone off to war. Croatia had become part of the new Kingdom of the Serbs, Croats and Slovenes (the name 'Yugoslavia' was only officially adopted in 1929), with other parts of the one-time Habsburg Monarchy (Slovenia, Dalmatia, Bosnia-Herzegovina, Voyvodina), and with the two independent states of Serbia and Montenegro.

Most of the territory was in confusion as the result of the war and of economic disruption. A combined central government had, right from the start, tackled the tasks of securing the frontiers and of redistributing the land. Otherwise, the political élites went on as if a united Yugoslav state were just Serbia writ large or a South Slav version of Austria-Hungary. The Constitution voted in 1921 updated the old Serbian model of a unitary state, with a parliamentary government under the Karadjordjević dynasty. Although passed by a slender majority, it was unacceptable to most Croats.

Serbs also played the leading part in uniting the revolutionary wings of the prewar Social-Democratic parties into a Yugoslav Communist movement. Sprung from the pro-Yugoslav tradition of South Slav socialists, they underestimated the real complexity of the new state's national question, yet expected that it would soon follow Russia into revolution. They were inspired by, and immediately joined, the Communist International, but the Comintern reduced Yugoslavia to a simple Serbian hegemony over non-Serbs, and just wanted to exploit what it judged to be a revolutionary situation.

The general strike called in July 1919 throughout Europe in protest against Allied intervention in Hungary and Russia was a challenge to the Yugoslav government — which had taken no

15

part in that intervention. The Communists had then gone on to reap over 12 per cent of the votes in the first Yugoslav general elections, in November 1920. They had been the first to organise themselves in all regions, and had skilfully exploited all manner of discontent. As they went on to threaten the disruption of fuel supplies with more strikes on the eve of the winter of 1920, and to turn to terrorism, the mood of the public towards them changed, thus enabling a nervous government to outlaw the Communist Party of Yugoslavia (KPJ) in July 1921.

The South Slav kingdom was beginning to settle both within its borders and in Europe. The multiplicity and diversity of parties represented in parliament continued to spell government by unstable coalitions, but the working classes were no longer responsive to Communist propaganda. The KPJ's initial successes had obscured its isolation, and it fell apart.

Tito had returned home with his Russian wife, twelve years his junior and pregnant, to learn that his mother had died, and that his father had moved to another village. They went to find him, Pelagija gave birth to a child who died after a few days, and Tito immediately left for Zagreb, never to see his father again. Three more children followed, of whom only a son, Žarko (1924), survived.

In spite of what he wrote later, Tito's police file shows no trace of militancy in the early 1920s. He rejoined his trade union, now incorporated into the KPJ, but his first employment seems to have been casual, perhaps as a waiter again. Early in 1921, he went to work in a flour mill, in a prosperous village north-west of Zagreb. It is difficult to say how he became politically conscious and active, but it could have been simply by adaptation to his milieu. In 1923 he responded positively when a former fellow-prisoner from Russia approached him to distribute leaflets for the Communist-influenced Independent Trade Unions, in effect recruiting him on probation for Party work. When his employer died in 1925, Tito was already being watched by the police, and the new owner told him he must choose between his job and his political activity.

He left, and for the next two years his employment was decided higher up, according to political needs. He thus worked in the

Kraljevica shipyard on the northern Adriatic, in the rail-carriage works at Smederevska Palanka in Serbia, and then was back in Zagreb in 1927 at a large engineering works. He turned from mechanic to paid Party official when it was decided that he should become secretary of the Metal Workers' Union of Croatia, one of the largest of the Independent Trade Unions, and of the Zagreb KPJ organisation. Pelagija was now also working for the Party. A few months later, at thirty-five, he had become secretary of the KPJ provincial committee when he was arrested for distributing illegal literature. A seven-month prison sentence was reduced on appeal, but in the mean time he had disappeared. When he was finally caught again in the summer of 1928, he was tried on more serious charges, and this time given a five-year term.

Reduced to less than 700 members in 1924 (compared with perhaps 120,000 in 1919), the KPJ had almost no influence over politics at that time, although it managed to survive through a Communist-inspired press and the Communist-operated but nominally Independent Trade Unions. Still basically an agglomeration of regional working-class groups, it was led by middle-class intellectuals — an ideal setting for factions arguing over who was responsible for the Party's collapse, and how to react to it.

Broadly defined as 'Right' and 'Left', the factions complained about each other to the Comintern, but were reluctant to accept its rulings. More purely Marxist, the Right dismissed the problem of Yugoslavia's national identities as being due to the bourgeoisies of its component parts having to compete on the expanded market of the new state — a problem that would disappear along with capitalism. More sceptical about illegal work and violence, it lost out to the Left as opportunities for legal action diminished. The Left was more Leninist in its quest for a revolutionary Party, firm in its ideology, but ready to adapt its tactics. It argued that the KPJ should give priority to the struggle against Serbian bourgeois nationalism, which interpreted Yugoslavia in a Serbian way.

The weakness of the KPJ made it increasingly dependent on the Comintern which, under Stalin, decided to use the revolutionary potential of nationalist and separatist movements. Having called for the dissolution of Yugoslavia at its 1924 World Congress, it increasingly intervened against the Right. As the KPJ was gradually being taken over by the Left, its activities moved from Belgrade to Zagreb. Distance from the central government, proximity to industrial areas, and a political atmosphere more and more hostile to the Yugoslav state establishment, made it a better base for Communist action.

Tito moves up in the Party

All this brought Tito closer to the top of the KPJ. He proved to be a good organiser in a propitious field of action — the Independent Trade Unions, whose strongest branches were in Croatia. Zagreb was the most industrialised urban area in Yugoslavia, with some 30,000 workers. When he was appointed head of the local Party organisation, Tito spoke out against factional disputes, and got his organisation to appeal to the Comintern to put an end to strife within the KPJ. This made a good impression in Moscow, and the Comintern used his appeal in order to intervene in May 1928 by means of an open letter which criticised both factions, extolled the Zagreb city Party, and announced the dismissal of the KPJ leadership.

In October, a Party Congress was convened in Dresden, Germany, where some thirty delegates assembled to listen to the Comintern line expounded by the Italian Communist Togliatti. They agreed that a rising of the oppressed nationalities would be the most efficient way of helping the Soviet Union if it were threatened by Western imperialists through Yugoslavia. A new leadership was elected. Factionalism was not yet at an end, but the KPJ was on its way to becoming an agency of agitators controlled from the outside.

That year, the parliamentary régime seemed to be grinding to a halt. After insults had been answered with revolver shots in parliament in June, mortally wounding the Croatian Peasant Party leader Radić, the atmosphere in Zagreb was tense. With Communist leaflets calling for a revolution to establish a Soviet republic, the police began an intensive search for known agitators, and Tito was finally apprehended.

His trial in November 1928 certainly brought him again to the notice of the Comintern. This time, bombs as well as explosive leaflets had been found in his lodging. Although his defence argued that they had been planted, he later admitted that he had hidden them on Party orders, as it was thought the time had come for armed struggle. Tito's defiant political statements also conformed to Party instructions and Comintern directives. He was sent to Lepoglava prison, in his native Zagorje, one of the penitentiaries where Communists were concentrated and no longer treated as ordinary convicts. They could meet, and were able to receive and borrow books. They created Party cells, organised courses of Marxist studies, and continued their feuds. Tito, who was put in charge of the electric plant, would later talk of Lepoglava as a 'university'. In 1931 he was transferred to Maribor in Slovenia, and finally freed in March 1934, having served his full term and more because of his first (1927) sentence.

Tito's time in prison coincided with the autocratic régime of King Alexander. On 6 January 1929, after four general elections and some twenty governments, the monarch decided he had had enough of parties and parliament, and dispensed with the Constitution of 1921 in order to prepare a better one. Yet, the parliamentary governments had governed; they had made a place for Yugoslavia in postwar Europe, and had put its economy in order. Agriculture had recovered, even though it still had to provide a living for too many people. Industry had been stimulated, in spite of steadfast faith in a mythical peasant way of life.

For the KPJ, the royal coup was proof that a revolutionary situation was at hand. It summoned the workers, peasants and oppressed nationalities to rise, but the response was nil. The new government banned the activity of all political parties, and closed down Communist-related publications and organisations. Armed revolt turned out to be no more than a series of shoot-outs with the police, which left the Party decimated and its leaders exiled and subject to annual replacement by the Comintern.

People were not sorry to have a respite from politics. The régime claimed it had saved the state, officially adopted the name Yugoslavia, and accelerated the pace of integration. But different sections of the population had expected different things from a temporary suspension of constitutional government. In 1931, when the full effect of the world economic crisis hit Yugoslavia and disappointment turned to unrest, the King granted a new Constitution which legalised his special powers. Having tried for three years to merge Serbian, Croatian and Slovenian feelings into one officially-inspired Yugoslav national identity, he was assassinated on 9 October 1934, at the start of a state visit to France. The assassin was a Macedonian agent of the secessionist Ustaša movement which had grown out of the radical fringe of Croatian dissatisfaction after 1929. On his release, Tito was required to reside in his native Kumrovec, but quickly went underground, and resumed his place in the Party hierarchy, living under assumed identities. It was then that he became 'Tito' —[1] the first (and, eventually, the last) of some seventy aliases he would use — and that he was sent to establish contact with KPJ headquarters, which were in Vienna.

The man in charge since 1932 was known as Milan Gorkić. Under him the Party was beginning to revive, moving away from senseless insurrection, towards infiltration of and agitation through legal organisations. Its activity, however, continued to be fraught with confusion and contradiction, not least because a leadership usually in Vienna acted as transmission between the Comintern in Moscow and militants in Yugoslavia. Both King Alexander's realm and his constitutionally veiled régime had survived him under the more flexible but less prestigious Prince Paul, who acted as regent for the boy King Peter II.

Back in Vienna after twenty years, Tito was in fact, if not formally, co-opted into the leadership. Now aged forty-two, he was hard-working, obedient, resourceful and with the right pedigree. His family life had stopped with his arrest. Pelagija had also spent some time in prison in 1928, and was then sent by the Party with her son to the Soviet Union, where she worked for the Comintern

---

[1] A common enough name in his area, from the Latin Titus, as in Italian. This is Tito's own simple explanation, which does away with the mysterious acronym TITO ('Third International Terrorist Organisation') and with the bossy derivative '*Ti — to*' ('You [do] that').

in Moscow, before going on to Kazakhstan as a teacher, committing Žarko to children's homes.

The revival was sufficiently advanced for a national Party conference to be held in Yugoslavia, and Tito was asked to help with its organisation. KPJ leaders from abroad joined eleven home delegates in December 1934 to elect a new permanent leadership, thus confirming Tito's co-option, and to continue the policy of encouraging those forces that favoured a break-up of Yugoslavia.

Party boss on probation

Tito had known for some time that Gorkić wanted him to go to Moscow, there to be trained for higher duties. He spoke both Russian and German, which was the second working language at the Comintern. Early in 1935, he was off, and was taken on as *referent* for the KPJ in the Balkan Secretariat of the Comintern, which had become a great administration in the service of Soviet foreign policy. He was in Russia again after fifteen years, although he had never before been in Moscow. His arrival coincided with the beginnings of Stalin's great purge whose implications, however, were not clear until after the end of the Comintern congress held that summer.

'Walter' — as Tito was henceforth called for Comintern purposes — lodged at the Hotel Lux, the residence assigned to all Comintern foreigners. He was, to all intents and purposes, free of family ties,[2] but kept safely to himself. He had always been able to adapt to his surroundings, and this he did again — from his romantic expectations to the stark realities of Moscow, from his previously assumed *persona* of a prosperous engineer to that of a quiet and industrious Party worker. He prepared memoranda on Yugoslav affairs, and lectured at Comintern educational establishments. The latter task made him read once again.

The seventh and last Comintern World Congress in August

---

[2] Pelagija, about whom he would say little to his biographers, remarried, had a daughter by her second husband, was caught up in the purges, exiled in 1938, and rehabilitated in 1957. In 1966 she returned to Moscow, where she died in 1968.

1935 made Communism in Europe dress itself in peace-loving and democratic clothes, as it proclaimed the new policy of a Popular Front against fascism. Tito attended as secretary to the KPJ delegation, and saw Stalin for the first time, at the formal opening. The line changed in Yugoslavia too: no longer to work for the country's break-up, but to press for its reorganisation on the basis of national equality. The KPJ did not find it easy. It failed to come to any agreement with the opposition parties, it was shaken by a formidable wave of arrests which undid much of what Gorkić had achieved, and it reverted to its quarrels.

The Comintern had to intervene yet again in the summer of 1936. Tito was sent to second Gorkić as organising secretary, with the double task of strengthening the Party at home and of recruiting volunteers to fight with the Republican army in the Spanish civil war. As KPJ headquarters moved to a more convenient location in Paris, Tito in 1937 travelled back and forth between there and Yugoslavia, having resumed his cover as a successful businessman.

The Spanish assignment was Tito's first experience of the West. With Comintern funds, he must have screened and channelled well over 1,000 Yugoslav volunteers, several hundred of them actually making their way from Yugoslavia. This was not easy, so it was decided to charter a ship to pick them up from a point on the Yugoslav coast. An operation of that size was difficult to conceal, the Yugoslav authorities intercepted it, and hundreds of volunteers were rounded up. The blame was pinned on Gorkić, and Tito was able to exculpate himself. Did he himself ever go to Spain? Rumours to that effect, including eye-witness reports, have accumulated since the late 1940s, and, while denying them, Tito never explained them away. Were they simply a case of mistaken identity, or did Tito have another, more confidential task — that of overseeing the liquidation in Spain of undesirable Communist dissidents?

The problem of Tito's participation in the purges, in Moscow and in Yugoslavia, also remains, and is linked to the manner of his taking over from Gorkić, about whom he probably knew by the end of 1936 that the Comintern had serious doubts. In a book published in Belgrade in 1989, Pero Simić has established eight different versions given by Tito over the years of how he came to be appointed by the Comintern to head the KPJ.[3] We now know that this was a long process, which lasted from the summer of 1937 to the autumn of 1940.

In July 1937, Gorkić was summoned from Paris to Moscow, never to return, one of the many victims of Stalin's purges. Two members of the Politbureau immediately asked Tito to come and take over, because only he could hold together the quarrelsome group in Paris. News was filtering through of the Moscow terror, and Tito found an atmosphere of panic among them when he returned from Yugoslavia. The struggle for the leadership was on. He started writing a stream of letters to Moscow — to explain that he had been asked to come and take over at the head of a caretaker leadership, to ask for guidance, and to urge that a regular leadership be formed in Yugoslavia. Moscow neither wrote back nor sent any money. Others in Paris were forming a rival centre, looking to Tito's competitor Petko Miletić who, though still in prison, had his followers and some support in the Comintern. At some stage, it was learnt in Paris that Gorkić had been found guilty of all sorts of crimes (including spying for the British), and that the whole KPJ leadership had been suspended.

With the Party situation in Yugoslavia deteriorating, Tito decided to return and establish his authority. In the spring of 1938, pending a decision to be taken in Moscow, he set up a provisional leadership around Djilas, Kardelj and Ranković, and was back in Paris in July. He had kept the Comintern informed of every step, and asked that he be allowed to come and explain. He was eventually summoned in August, but was not received by Dimitrov, the secretary-general of the Comintern, until the autumn, and then only to be given a dressing-down for all the past sins of the KPJ.

Was the Yugoslav Communist organisation even worth keeping in existence? A special Comintern working party was looking into the matter, and no decision was taken until the New Year.

---

[3] *Kad, kako i zašto je Tito postavljen za sekretara CK KPJ*, Belgrade: Aquarius, 1989.

Meanwhile Tito was back at the Lux, whose population had been thinned out. He had been told to help with the Serbo-Croatian translation of Stalin's *Short History of the Bolshevik Party*, and he was also busy writing reports for the Comintern. On 5 January 1939, the Comintern's Executive Committee finally came up with its decision: it approved of what Tito had done, and formally entrusted him with the temporary leadership for three months. He was to prove himself by consolidating the KPJ according to the wishes of the Comintern, which meant purging it of all unsuitable elements. After careful reflection it had decided that a reactivated KPJ was probably more useful than no KPJ at all, and that the only suitable Yugoslav to reactivate it was Tito.

He was the type of the new generation of leaders emerging from the great purge. He was not associated with any particular clique, had not come up through the Social Democrats, and was no intellectual. He knew when and how to take the initiative, and was loyal to Moscow. Stalin's terror had already begun to affect the Comintern when Tito was there in 1936, but he had kept quiet about what he saw. He had justified the Moscow trials in KPJ literature, and had written reports on Yugoslav comrades — which was usual practice.

The full story of the purge of Yugoslavs in the Soviet Union may never be known, since Tito was one of the few to escape with his life. Dedijer estimates that some 800 Yugoslav Communists were liquidated at that time, but Tito was discreet to the end. His apparent confusion about the manner and time of his appointment is now explained in Belgrade as a way of covering up his role in the purges, although it is unlikely that his reports (the contents of which are not known) were decisive in sending comrades to their death.

He left Moscow in late January 1939 and returned to Yugoslavia in March by way of Paris. Dimitrov had to intervene with the French Communist Party to help him wind up and silence the headless KPJ leadership in Paris. Tito could thus firmly locate it again in Yugoslavia. Without delay he called together his provisional leadership, and took a number of decisions. All the 'criminal activities' discovered since 1937 were denounced. All those who had been arrested in the Soviet Union were expelled. A conference would be called as soon as possible to reorganise the KPJ on the Soviet model.

Tito certainly did not start from scratch. Had he wanted to, he would not have found it particularly easy, as he did not yet have full control. He took over a party that had already begun to pick up, that could capitalise on resentment against the semi-authoritarian and quasi-parliamentarian régime of the Regency, and that was freeing itself from factionalism, but one that would henceforth be constricted by Stalinist precepts and tactics.

He continued with the task of building up a new organisation, with young revolutionaries hardened in fieldwork and free from the mutual distrust, the local connections and the police records of their elders. He had been ordered to carry out a thorough purge of the Party, and he certainly wielded his broom to get rid of personalities tied to his rival Miletić, or who expressed loyalty to former factions or acted independently. As he and the new leadership were not yet in a position to enforce their orders overnight, the purge, to the point of physical elimination, would go on during the war.

Tito had managed to extend his three-month probation until August, when he went to Moscow for a review of his stewardship. This was his last visit there before the war, and it lasted four months. By the time of his arrival, the German-Soviet Pact had been signed. By the time that he reported, Poland had been attacked and the Second World War had started. In November, the Executive Committee of the Comintern endorsed his report, and confirmed in principle his appointment as political secretary of the KPJ's Central Committee. It was still subject to his dealing 'as soon as possible' with some remaining shortcomings: his purges had not been thorough enough, work in the trade unions and in rural areas was slack, and Party organisation was not quite up to the mark.

Apparently, this was the time when Tito most feared that he would not come out alive, but he had made sufficient progress towards accomplishing the tasks assigned to him. He returned, after a long voyage by way of Istanbul, where he stayed for three months, awaiting convincingly forged papers (but perhaps also the Party courier Herta Has, a twenty-six-year old Slovenian economics graduate of Austrian origin whom he had met in Paris). In March 1940 he was back in Zagreb, eager to get down to preparing the KPJ conference, or rather the congress, which would both affirm the revolutionary strategy based on the Soviet model, and impress Moscow.

Tito worked overtime. He felt comfortable with the current Comintern line of class war and new-style Popular Front from below, combined with propaganda in favour of the Soviet Union as the defender of small countries against imperialists. By September he felt confident enough to send an emissary to Moscow to report on how he had eliminated remaining shortcomings, and on preparations for the forthcoming congress. On 15 October, the Comintern's Executive Committee finally gave its full approval. Both Tito and his new Central Committee were confirmed, but he was warned against too much enthusiasm. He should hold a conference rather than a fully-fledged congress so as to avoid taking risks with the police, and he should tone down any call for the dictatorship of the proletariat so as not to provoke the imperialist powers. Only if and when Yugoslavia became the victim of an unprovoked aggression should the KPJ go for revolution.

The Comintern's anointed

The all-Yugoslav Conference was duly held four days later, from 19 to 23 October 1940. Although not called a congress, it was Tito's final consecration. Over 100 delegates gathered clandestinely in a house in a Zagreb suburb and, representing just under 6,500 members, once again duly constituted the KPJ as a fully structured section of the Comintern under Tito's leadership. Presenting himself as enjoying Moscow's full confidence, he stigmatised all his predecessors, and described the 'second imperialist war' as one between two rival blocks of capitalist powers. The Party did not want Yugoslavia to be dragged in, but it should be ready for all eventualities.

Political developments in Yugoslavia in the late 1930s had resulted not in a Popular Front, but in the tightening-up of the existing alliance of Croatian and Serbian opposition parties. The United Opposition had made headway in elections, in spite of a system designed to favour the government, until August 1939, when the Croatian Peasant Party alone had come to an agreement with the régime to set up a self-governing Province of Croatia. The Croatian compromise had been made under pressure of foreign events, with the Regency veering to a policy of neutrality. The growing strength of Germany and Italy made that neutrality difficult, particularly after the fall of France in June 1940. As German pressure increased, the Yugoslav government eventually caved in, and on 25 March 1941 it joined the 'satellites', only to be overthrown two days later.

Meanwhile the KPJ had achieved some successes. It had extended its organisation to areas where it had not existed before. It had become to a large extent self-contained and self-supporting, yet linked to a powerful protector abroad. Tito has too often been given sole credit for a resurgence which had started when he was still mostly abroad and not yet fully in charge, and even before that, under Gorkić. Reorganisation and expansion were the work of many hands, not least those of Kardelj, Ranković and Djilas who, with Tito, had formed something of a quadrumvirate since 1938.

Tito had the authority naturally assumed by one who was the Comintern's anointed. His position was strengthened by the fact that every individual who had been important previously had been removed, and that the new team he had selected was made up of younger men for whom he was a father-figure ('*Stari*', the Old Man). Although policies were worked out collectively, he was the final arbiter of the interpretation and execution in Yugoslavia of a line received from Moscow, and he demanded unquestioning loyalty.

The new generation of militants lived psychologically outside society in a secret fraternity that was to become their family, their nation and their church, with indoctrination courses, a code of conduct and a Party inquisition to enforce it. Membership had increased from 1,500 in 1937 to an estimated 8,000 in 1941, which, even allowing for some exaggeration, certainly indicated a healthy growth.

Recruitment and promotion followed strict Comintern procedures and put special emphasis on youth. This was more successful in the student milieu than on the shop-floor, let alone the villages. Political activity was free within universities, whose autonomy was always respected by the régime which had otherwise both depoliticised and radicalised the educated young. One of the historians of the KPJ, Ivan Avakumović, reminds us nevertheless that in 1939 Belgrade University had more students but fewer Communist Party members than Cambridge.

After the defeat and failure of the Popular Front experiments in Spain and France, the KPJ could claim with some justification to have become something of a model, a claim reinforced by the Comintern's decision to base in Zagreb its new radio-transmitter for communications with other Communist parties of central and south-eastern Europe. The Soviet-German Pact was accepted and defended by its clandestine press, which denounced the Western imperialists as the aggressors. Fully aligning itself with the Soviet position, the KPJ had been given the assignment to keep Yugoslavia neutral, thus reflecting Moscow's desire to stop the Balkans falling into either camp.

By the beginning of 1941, it had become a Bolshevik-type party under Tito — a closely-knit revolutionary group, unshakable in its devotion to the Soviet Union, which it praised as a model for solving all Yugoslavia's problems. Living in the dream-world of the Communist society of the future and in expectation of a revolution, its achievements had increasingly been made at the cost of some isolation from mainstream popular feelings. The ever-greater virulence of its anti-war and anti-defence agitation had not only led the government to revert to some control measures at the end of 1939; it was also driving a wedge between young Communists and Western-inclined groups among young oppositionists.

When it decided to adhere to the Tripartite Pact, the Regency had already antagonised a substantial portion of the population, particularly among the Serbs. Tension was such that the officers' coup of 27 March probably forestalled a revolt or disorders of sorts, which was what Tito had been expecting, but the Communist leadership knew nothing of the coup in advance. Caught off-guard, it could only join in the demonstrations, adding calls for an alliance with Moscow. Once again, the Comintern cautioned the Party against getting carried away, since the final reckoning was still a long way off.

The coup brought together the leaders of all the parliamentary parties in a broad coalition government. It showed a deep yearning not so much for a revolution as for a fully representative government in an hour of need, but it could only paper over the differences between the various political conceptions it encompassed. Although the new cabinet did begin to release Communist prisoners and internees, and although it did conclude a treaty with the Soviet Union, it was never given time to sort out a policy. Attacked by Hitler on 6 April 1941, Yugoslavia was stunned and put out of action in less than a fortnight.

The common enterprise of the South Slavs would have been a difficult one, even if attempted in the best possible conditions. As it was, the abnormal strains created by the multiplicity of traditions, the world economic crisis and the appearance of totalitarian ideologies imposed impossible burdens on the somewhat clumsy grouping together of diverse regions in imitation of West European forms.

The Communists had swum in all the tides, and got themselves terribly entangled until Tito appeared at the eleventh hour to give the Party some cohesion. With the blessing of, and occasional words of caution from, the Comintern, he Bolshevised the KPJ and made it ready to seize the opportunity the Second World War would offer. He had known how to initiate in Yugoslavia his own interpretation of the Comintern line. With its cadres of devoted and capable professional revolutionaries, the Party was far stronger in 1941 than it had been in 1937, but it could not have taken power if the war and occupation had not destroyed the political and social structure of Yugoslavia.

3

THE WAR YEARS, 1941–1945:
INSURGENT AND REVOLUTIONARY

Revolution under occupation: 1941

Following the rapid conquest of its territory, Yugoslavia was shared out between the Axis powers (Germany and Italy) and their satellites (Hungary, Bulgaria and Albania). In addition, the Ustašas were allowed to set up a greater 'Independent State of Croatia' (NDH), which took in Bosnia and Herzegovina and became part of the Nazi-Fascist New Order.

Early in May, Tito got together some of his lieutenants. He told them that bourgeois Yugoslavia was dead, that the break-up of the Nazi-Soviet Pact was on the cards, soon to be followed by Germany's defeat, and that the KPJ should brace itself to seize power in alliance with the Soviet Union. The leadership would be transferred to Belgrade, where conditions were better under German military rule than in Zagreb under Ustaša police surveillance. Leaving behind Herta, with whom he had been living, and who was about to give birth to a son, Aleksandar (Miša), Tito started a new liaison in Belgrade with a twenty-year-old student, Davorjanka (Zdenka) Paunović, who remained with him until 1944.[1]

During the ambiguous period that preceded Hitler's attack on the Soviet Union, Tito worked hard to maintain the cohesion of the KPJ, until the invasion of Russia on 22 June 1941 at last provided the expected conditions for a rising. The Party hierarchy turned itself into a military chain of command when enjoined by the Comintern to start 'partisan' action. Tito sent emissaries to various parts, but himself stayed in Belgrade where the victorious Russians were expected.

---

[1] Captured by the Germans and released in 1943 as a result of a prisoner exchange, Herta joined the partisans in Slovenia, reappeared briefly at Jajce, where she quarrelled with Zdenka, and married (someone else) after the war.

It was on 12 July that he summoned the population to come to the aid of the Soviet Union, but that summer there were in fact no less than three separate and spontaneous risings. Hitler blamed the Serbs for all the troubles in the Balkans, and they alone were formally treated as a vanquished foe. The insurgents were thus practically all Serbs, and they went by the traditional name of chetniks (*četnik*).

It was the Ustašas' ferocious racism that forced the Orthodox Serbs in their greater Croatia to fight for their lives. The population of Montenegro, which was generally Serbian in feeling, resisted the Italian attempt to set up a client-state. In Serbia itself, an upsurge of pro-Allied enthusiasm produced a revolt against the Germans. There, a group of army officers under Colonel Mihailović was already trying to organise a resistance movement loyal to the King and the government that had taken refuge in London, when Tito took the opportunity to rouse the peasants against the local representatives of the old government machine.

After the 1948 break, Tito's apologists tried to read the differences with Moscow at least back to 1941. Differences in perspective there were, and they could not be bridged easily because of the breakdown in direct communications. Between April and June, the Soviet government did consider accepting the fact of Yugoslavia's partition. Tito's control over a KPJ bewildered by the pace of events was not as great as he wanted the Soviets to believe; he had problems with separatist tendencies in Croatia and Macedonia; and his various appeals to unite against the invaders did not yet specifically endorse a united Yugoslavia. Moscow wanted maximum diversion in the Germans' rear rather than preparation for a revolutionary seizure of power, but it must have been pleased with any guerrilla action, even with Tito's mixture of sabotage and revolution, and even with Mihailović's action for King and country.

In Montenegro the Communists were carried on a surge which they could not control, and which floundered as soon as the Italians brought in reinforcements from Albania and let loose Albanian and Muslim auxiliaries. The peasants went home, fearing for their families. The officers, who had played a large part in the revolt, concluded that it was premature. The local Communists tried to keep it going by seeking revenge on 'traitors'.

It would take several months for that sort of rivalry to turn to civil war in Serbia, where Tito was directly in charge of his Party activists. Concerned over the different way in which Communist action was developing from region to region, troubled about the need to make some deal with Mihailović, and finding it increasingly difficult to keep up contacts from Belgrade, he left the capital on 16 September. The KPJ was, however, still psychologically wedded to the idea of gaining power through the cities, and Tito's headquarters were set up in Užice as soon as the Germans had withdrawn from that Serbian town. As the 'Užice Republic', it immediately came to symbolise the beginnings of the new Communist order.

Tito's first task was to see Mihailović on 19 September, but the meeting was inconclusive. Both aimed at taking control, on behalf of the Communist revolution and of the legitimate government respectively, and neither anticipated seriously tackling the Germans until the occupiers' power had started to crumble. Tito then went to a gathering of Party leaders on 26–27 September, when it was decided to stimulate uprisings everywhere so as to create areas under Communist rule, but to avoid fighting with enemy troops.

The Germans soon took measures. As they could not afford to bring in reinforcements from other theatres for more than a short time, they terrorised the population of Serbia into submission. The Communist-led partisans, who appeared to continue with indiscriminate action irrespective of reprisals, became unpopular, and their relations with the officer-led chetniks took a turn for the worse, although Tito and Mihailović did meet once again at the end of October.

After consulting together one last time, over the telephone, Mihailović decided to disperse his formations and lie low, and Tito decided to move out of the Germans' way into the rugged region that separates Serbia from Montenegro. The Italians had given it up to winter cold and roaming armed bands, and the Germans did not pursue the partisans there, but the situation was dire.

As the retreating Communist leaders met to take stock, they heard that the *Wehrmacht* had been stopped before Moscow, and Tito's optimism was rekindled. Once again, he was convinced of Hitler's imminent downfall, to be accompanied by the collapse of the unnatural anti-fascist coalition. That meant an end to any co-operation with the class enemy at home, and an all-out struggle against reactionaries and anglophiles. Slow to fathom the extent of popular revulsion against the partisans, he attributed it to the machinations of the 'English', the villains of capitalist imperialism.

The partisans reforged their unity at the cost of ruthlessly eliminating all those who were judged unreliable, and went on to the remote highlands of south-eastern Bosnia. There the chetniks had the upper hand, but they were ready enough to welcome Tito's 'Serbian army'. Some 1,200 of the original Communist partisans who had retreated from Serbia and Montenegro were organised into the First Proletarian People's Liberation Brigade on 21 December — Stalin's birthday. They were the first of five such units to be formed over the following six months as shock troops of the KPJ, imbued with Party dogma and discipline, and ready to be sent anywhere to fight for the revolution. The others, the ordinary insurgents and new recruits who would have felt revulsion at becoming Communist fighters, were formed into 'volunteer detachments', and it was death to all who remained under independent chieftains.

The symbols of international Communism were prominently displayed; Communist propaganda was instilled into all fighters and disseminated everywhere; Stalin was extolled as the only real anti-fascist leader, but so was Tito as his prophet in Yugoslavia.[2] Regional commands and cadres were told of the need for action to keep up the momentum, to avoid Italian troops, and to go for chetniks and class enemies. Whether or not Tito had sought

---

[2] Dedijer in his diary quotes partisan marching songs of the time, such as: 'O, Stalin, people's god — without you we could not live', or 'With Tito and Stalin, two heroic beings — even Hell cannot confound us'. He also records that Tito wept for joy and pride when he learnt that his son Žarko, who served in the Red Army, had been decorated after losing an arm in the battle for Moscow.

genuine co-operation with Mihailović in 1941, from now on he would work relentlessly for his destruction.

The result was catastrophic for the partisans. In Montenegro, it led to them being effectively driven out, and to the chetniks settling for some sort of power-sharing with the Italians until the early summer of 1943. Although Communists there were rebuked for their excesses by Tito, who never showed any bloodthirsty tendencies himself, the alleged 'Left' deviation went on into 1942, particularly in the areas of the independent state of Croatia (NDH) adjacent to Montenegro. The Italian military won over local chetniks by offering the Serbian population protection against the Ustašas, while partisans hit out at 'kulaks', looting and burning 'chetnik' villages.

Throughout that winter of retreat, terror was not just for the class enemy, as Ranković and his security organisation rooted out 'henchmen of the British' among the partisans, punished demoralisers who said the struggle would be long and hard, and continued the Party purges initiated by Tito before the war. Further west, there had been very little real partisan activity among Croats, as they did not have to go out and resist, and as KPJ strength had been concentrated in industrial centres now well controlled by the Ustaša régime. In Slovenia, the Communists' militancy had led to the loss of their original initiative and the consolidation of the hold of the Catholic party. Only in western Bosnia were the partisans still strong enough to make it possible for the KPJ to take the lead of a popular movement.

The Party under Tito followed its own dynamism in 1941. It could not do much to defeat Hitler's armies in Russia, but it believed it could do much to advance the Communist order in Yugoslavia now that the old kingdom had been destroyed, and there were no more than three or four German divisions in the country. The same reasons that made Mihailović withdraw into a wait-and-see attitude made Tito go for revolution at a time when no one in the wider world knew what was going on in Yugoslavia.

East to West: Bosnia, 1942

Left to their own devices in 1942, the insurgents survived by mimesis and mobility — by moving about, by blending into or hiding behind the scenery. Mihailović prepared for a rising to be launched when the Allies were near enough to make it worthwhile. The first guerrilla leader in Nazi-occupied Europe, he had been built up in the West into the hero of the Yugoslav resistance. Promoted general by the government in exile, which appointed him its war minister, he also tried to bind together all those forces outside Serbia that could strengthen his own movement — the Yugoslav Home Army.

The Serbian rebels in the NDH who had welcomed the Italians' protection were also anxious to legitimise their position in the eyes of the population by acknowledging General Mihailović. He gambled on being able to bring them under his effective command, and he lost, for he never had any real authority over these chetniks, who were increasingly dependent on the Italians. This made it easier for Tito's movement to emerge again in western Yugoslavia.

Having established himself in January at Foča, in south-eastern Bosnia, Tito resumed direct radio contact with 'Grandad' — the code-name for Dimitrov. He admitted his critical situation and begged for aid, but also claimed that he had a force of 200,000 active and organised combatants, much of which (as he later admitted to Phyllis Auty) 'existed only on paper'. He was no less generous in providing Moscow with details of his rivals' misdeeds and of British intrigues.

There was not much that the Soviets could do for him at this time. They told the British and Yugoslav governments that they had no authority to ask the partisans to join Mihailović. They stopped mentioning Mihailović in their media. Otherwise, they had to break it gently to Tito that technical difficulties prevented material aid from being sent to him in the near future.

Flatteringly, Moscow told him that his movement set a heroic example to occupied Europe, but impressed upon him that the successful defence of Moscow did not herald the immediate arrival of the Red Army in Yugoslavia. He was advised to refrain from anything which could endanger the Allied Coalition against Hitler, and to disguise the obvious Communist character of his partisans. He was to understand that his protectors could not yet afford to be seen protecting him, and he was to provide hard facts to be used in building up a case against Mihailović. Stalin's top priority was the survival of the Soviet Union, for which he needed Western aid. He feared that lend-lease deliveries might be jeopardised, that preparations for a second front would be delayed, and even that the West might do a deal with Germany.

The KPJ leadership gathered again around Tito to take stock of Moscow's advice, and of the domestic situation. Expectations of early liberation could no longer be sustained, and the radical stance had alienated the peasants on whom the Party's struggle for post-war power depended. A new double line was elaborated: the broader line of the People's Liberation Struggle against the occupying powers, as the means of enlisting non-Communist patriots around the KPJ and damning all who refused it, and the narrower line of class warfare and Communist hegemony within the broader one. It could be summed up as: 'Who is not against us is potentially with us, until we decide otherwise'.

Stalin's priorities allowed Tito some freedom in domestic affairs. He naturally accepted that the interests of the Soviet Union, as the ultimate guarantor of the Yugoslav revolution, were paramount, and that Stalin knew best how to defend them, but he continued to be obsessively distrustful of the British. He made it explicit in his orders that, while the Grand Alliance — not only Russia, but the Anglo-Saxon powers as well — should be stressed publicly, the KPJ would continue to strike at the latter's 'hangers-on and agents as lackeys of the occupiers and enemies of the people'.

The Italians had woken up to the danger of allowing Tito's force to expand in the Foča area, and anyway that devastated triangle of Bosnia between Serbia and Montenegro could no longer support it. Thus it was decided in mid-June to take to another no-man's-land, in north-western Bosnia on the borders of inner Croatia, where headquarters would be set up in November.

That 'long march' took 3,000 or so partisans along the wooded mountainous watershed that formed the boundary between the German and Italian zones of Yugoslavia, and it did much to restore their image. The region had been fought over by Ustašas, out for Serbian blood, and by chetniks, out for revenge, with Muslims in between, but the mixed population was, on the whole, neutral to the partisans. Tito avoided Axis troops, withdrew when pursued, and entered into mutually convenient arrangements with small enemy garrisons. His partisans were greeted as protectors by the decimated Serbian population, but although mostly Serbs themselves, they were careful to prevent hatred of the Ustašas from turning against Croats generally, and were always on the side of those who were fighting for their lives (unless those happened to be marked as political enemies). Their reputation went ahead of them, and helped them through Catholic and Muslim areas.

The original partisans from Serbia were not too happy about going off to a remote and primitive region where the KPJ had never developed. Tito knew that Serbia was the key to victory, and he was aware of the weakness of the Communist position in Bosnia, but he now realised that there was no early prospect of restoring any influence in Serbia, and he guessed that the Serbs of the western territories would eagerly welcome leadership from whatever quarter it came. 'This is the shortest route back to Serbia,' he told his commanders.

'The Western Serbs were Tito's last refuge, they became the basis from which to conquer all Yugoslavia.'[3] Bosnia became the bastion of the partisan movement. Having forged a mobile and disciplined fighting force, and advocating religious and ethnic tolerance, Tito penetrated the desperate struggle against extermination of the Orthodox Serbs of the NDH. His movement throve on the anarchy of the Ustaša state, as young Croats in their turn came to escape conscription and possible service in Russia,

[3] F. Borkenau, *European Communism*, London: Faber and Faber, 1953, p. 372.

thus spearheading a more general turning away from the NDH. By infiltrating its administration and army, the Communists also obtained valuable support and useful intelligence.

In western Bosnia there were no Axis troops, the NDH was weak, and Mihailović was too distant to be of consequence. By the autumn, the territory controlled by the partisans is usually said to have been the size of Switzerland, with Tito's headquarters at Bihać. By taking them out of their respective milieux, the KPJ was transforming the adolescents of Bosnia into combatants of supranational units of the People's Liberation Army (NOV), whose cadres were made up of partisans who had come from the east. Under Tito as supreme commander, this force had increased threefold since leaving Foča, and continued to grow over the winter.

Unobserved by the Allies and ignored by the chetniks, who believed that the partisan adventure had definitely collapsed, Tito also turned to broadening the apparent basis of his movement. The KPJ leadership wanted a platform from which to rally non-Communist patriots, and to challenge the exiled government. Tito consulted the Comintern about his intention to set up 'something like a government'. Moscow approved of an all-Yugoslav body that would look broadly anti-fascist, but not yet of a counter-government.

On 26 November 1942, some fifty pre-selected decoys, puppets and fellow-travellers met at Bihać as the Anti-Fascist Council for the National Liberation of Yugoslavia (AVNOJ) — the 'parliament' of the People's Liberation Movement. An elderly non-Communist Croat who had been president of the Constituent Assembly after the First World War, and had now been smuggled out of Belgrade to join his Communist sons, was elected chairman of AVNOJ. A manifesto was issued, which proclaimed that the People's Liberation Movement harnessed all true patriots to the task of liberating Yugoslavia, and of restoring it as the democratic state of all its inhabitants. It was meant to give the impression that it was an expression of forward-looking patriotism, not an instrument of Communist revolution. Outside it, however, were only traitors and collaborators.

Tito was at its centre, already the object of a cult,[4] wrapped up in some mystery, which was still great outside the ranks of the partisans. Wild rumours circulated as to his true identity. In his speech to AVNOJ he stressed that it had all been achieved through faith in the might of the Soviet Union, and such professions were the stuff of partisan propaganda. 'Our allies' England and America did appear, but less often and less prominently than 'our Great Ally' Soviet Russia. The climax was reached in the article published for the anniversary of the Bolshevik Revolution that year, where Stalin was glorified as the faultless human being 'without whom the sun would have been darkened'.

The Soviet Union, still fighting for its life, continued to caution Tito against too enthusiastic protestations of love, and to ask him to give more prominence to the Grand Alliance, but such preoccupations were still difficult for the KPJ leadership to understand; they were still novices in international relations. By the summer, however, Moscow had gone so far as to provide the Yugoslav government, and the Communist press around the world, with arguments against Mihailović. From the autumn, it also gave Tito the tremendous propaganda support of a powerful transmitter, Radio Free Yugoslavia, which, although in the Soviet Union, purported to be somewhere in partisan territory.

West-East return: Bosnia, 1943

Outside interest in Yugoslavia increased at the end of 1942, when the victories in North Africa opened the way for an assault on 'Fortress Europe'. As the Allies gave more importance to diversionary action in the Balkans, the Germans were anxious to suppress all insurgents. In fact, the operation they launched in January 1943 against the partisan concentration in western Bosnia merely anticipated Tito's intended return to the south-east in order to defeat his rivals before the Allies landed.

By quickly getting out of their way, and by exploiting German-

---

[4] The famous song had already appeared: 'Comrade Tito, we swear to you that we shall not deviate from your path'.

Italian tensions and his links with the NDH, Tito once again managed to save his forces. The operations of January–March were a military defeat for him, but gave no lasting victory to the Axis. During that time, Tito and Mihailović also fought desperately for control of the southern Adriatic hinterland, each anxious to destroy the other before the expected British landing. This led to an increasing entanglement of antagonisms and arrangements, as Tito approached the Germans to arrange a cease-fire.

His negotiators, led by Djilas, offered to stop harassing the Axis if the partisans were allowed to return to their homes or go and fight the chetniks, who were anyway their main enemies and whom they denounced as being both tolerated by the Italians and linked to the British. They even envisaged joint defensive action with the Germans in case of an Allied landing.

Tito in March was in a desperate situation. His main combatant group of some 20–40,000 was accompanied by at least as many refugees. Hard-pressed by an Axis ring closing in on three sides, he faced roughly the same number of chetniks who were concentrating in Herzegovina to stop the partisans, and hoping that the Germans would destroy them. The Germans did call a halt to their anti-partisan drive, as Tito suspended guerrilla operations against them. He thus gained a respite, which made it easier for the partisans to win a difficult victory over the chetniks in Herzegovina and Montenegro.

The battle of the Neretva, Tito's controversial crossing of that deep valley, had enabled the bulk of the partisan force to slip out of the ring into the uplands of Montenegro and engage in savage battles with the chetniks. Taken off-guard by the resumption of the Germans' anti-insurgent offensive after the failure of the talks, he had to stop any further penetration eastward, and make his way again to eastern Bosnia, through mountains slashed by gorges, exposed to the full pressure of Axis operations after he and the Germans had done their best to destroy the chetnik screen.

Eventually, by the end of June, he had made good his escape with his staff and a force shrunk to some 10,000. Important things had been happening as he was disentangling himself. In May he had been told that the Comintern would cease its activities as a gesture to reassure the Allies, but this made no difference to the KPJ. Dimitrov's machinery remained as the International Department of the Soviet Party Central Committee, and Tito still referred to it as the 'Comintern'. He continued to report to Grandad, who continued to let him act as he knew best in Yugoslavia, within broad guidelines, so long as he did not upset the Anglo-Americans.

The latter had invaded Italy in June, which made it necessary to exploit all opportunities of involving the enemy on the other side of the Adriatic. The British were thus demanding of Mihailović more than he was able or willing to give without adequate support, and turning to Tito as an additional or alternative source of support. Advance liaison teams had already been dropped into partisan territory before a mission arrived at Tito's headquarters at the end of May under F.W.D. (later Sir William) Deakin, an Oxford don who had helped Churchill with his writings before the war.

Although he was ever suspicious, and his entourage were convinced that the capitalists were preparing to destroy the partisans with the help of the chetniks under the cover of liberation by Allied troops, Tito was quick to take advantage of British exasperation with Mihailović. He and his staff were also lucky in being able to impress the well-connected chief of mission with the partisans' valour and ability to recover.

Deakin's reports made an impact. Communist propaganda, left-wing tendencies, the discord within the Yugoslav government in London, and a confused understanding of what was happening in Yugoslavia also contributed to an opinion being formed in British policy-making circles that to support the partisans could help remove Soviet suspicions of Western intentions, and make Tito responsive to advice from London. By the time that Italy had been removed from the war at the end of the summer, the head of the KPJ had replaced General Mihailović as hero of the Yugoslav resistance.

Back in its earlier base in eastern Bosnia, Tito's movement increasingly benefited from the demoralisation of the Ustaša régime throughout the territory of the NDH. It extended its political activity. Croats too were going over to the partisans, especially among the military who could expect no mercy from exclusively Serbian and nationalist chetniks. As the KPJ organisation strengthened again in Croatia, however, it tended to put more emphasis on Croatia than on Yugoslavia, which created unease among the Serbs there who had suffered under the Ustašas, and had been the first to join the partisans. This was a tricky situation, which Tito sent Djilas to look into.

Another region which attracted Tito's attention in 1943 was Macedonia, where neither he nor Mihailović had had much success, but which he regarded as potentially favourable terrain in view of local resentment against Bulgarian rule. The Comintern had come out in favour of the KPJ over Macedonia. Tito despatched there another of his lieutenants, Svetozar Vukmanović-Tempo, to work for a united Slav Macedonia under Yugoslav Communist auspices, and to establish contact with Albanian, Greek and Bulgarian Communists. It seems that Tempo was a little too overt in setting up a Balkan headquarters to spread KPJ influence. Tito had to bring that particular venture to an end in September, but he still told his emissary that he (and the Comintern) thought Yugoslavia would continue to play a major role in the Balkans.

The collapse of Italy in September brought a huge accession of matériel to the partisans, a moral boost and a sudden, if temporary, expansion of territory. Tito, however, was not alone in counting on Italian spoils, and Mihailović, who had engaged in only limited activity against the Germans since the end of 1941, emerged again in the latter half of 1943 to the point where he is estimated to have led the second-most active resistance movement in Europe, after Tito's.

That is why Tito was furious with the British for not having given him advance notice of the Italian armistice. Nevertheless, most of those who wanted to find themselves with the Allies in the Italian zone threw in their lot with the partisans, who were able to turn against the distinctly weaker chetniks as the Germans turned against the Italians.

The partisan movement then became militarily stronger than

all other native armed formations, and along with it grew the power of the KPJ. Tito's manifest intention of ruling Yugoslavia encountered little resistance from the Allies, much to Stalin's surprise. In order to get more out of him, the Anglo-Americans came to accept Tito's view that his People's Liberation Movement was not just the more effective resistance, but the only one.

Once he had found a 'capital' again in the central Bosnian town of Jajce, it seemed to Tito and the KPJ leadership that the time had come to complete the institutionalisation of the movement that had been started at Bihać. An extended AVNOJ of 142 Communists and fellow-travellers assembled for a second congress on 29 November 1943. Speeches made in the presence of the British mission (who probably did not understand them) referred to twenty years of oppression endured under a handful of greater-Serbian hegemonists, and to the traitors whose leaders were still recognised by 'our allies' and enjoying their hospitality. A series of motions was adopted that virtually set up a new Yugoslav state. Although final decisions would be made by the people after the war, AVNOJ II denied the exiled government any rights, forbade the King to return, assumed legislative functions, and gave its National Committee for the Liberation of Yugoslavia the character of a provisional government. Federalism was postulated as the principle according to which the country would be organised.

Tito was made president of the National Committee, and given the rank of marshal of a partisan army, aping Soviet forms. At fifty-one he was already the object of a cult, propagated by the KPJ as a subsidiary to that of Stalin. He was a natural phenomenon destined to sweep away fascist invaders and oppressors. He was assimilated in song and verse to the country's geography and flora.[5] With his supreme military rank, he was made the equal of other great war leaders and of the rulers of old, as conceived by popular imagination. British propaganda contributed greatly to his cult from the autumn of 1943 onwards.

He was careful to inform Moscow in advance of the AVNOJ

---

[5] 'Tito, the earth and the river', or the more famous and long-enduring 'Tito, little white violet'.

decisions, but in a way that would minimise the chances of their being down-graded. At the last moment, he told Dimitrov of the proposed transformation of AVNOJ into the base for a new government in Yugoslavia, and asked him to bring this to the attention of the foreign ministers then meeting in Moscow to prepare for the Tehran Conference. He also claimed that he had been told by the head of the British mission that London would not insist on supporting the King and his government. Initially irritated, as he feared this would upset his negotiations with the Allies, Stalin quickly realised that no opposition was forthcoming, and that the world press assumed that the Jajce decisions had been taken in agreement with the Big Three.

At Tehran Churchill, Roosevelt and Stalin agreed to give all possible help to the partisans in Yugoslavia: Tito had profited from the desire of both the Russians and the Anglo-Americans not to oppose each other in a lesser and uncertain sphere before the major victories had been won.

To power via Vis and Moscow: 1944

By the time the Western Allies had definitely turned to Tito, their advance had slowed down in Italy, and the Germans had recovered their balance in Yugoslavia. Partisan headquarters had had to move back to western Bosnia, where at Drvar, in February 1944, Tito donned his new marshal's uniform to welcome a high-ranking Soviet military mission of generals and colonels come to join British and American representatives.

He also sent Djilas with a mission to Moscow — formally justified as a counterpart to the partisans' military mission to Algiers and London. He was to show how good the Yugoslav Communists had been, and obtain rewards in the shape of aid and political recognition. He was told that the Soviet government would ask the British for an air base in Italy through which they could channel aid. He was also told that he would do well to accept Churchill's idea of talks with Šubašić, the Croatian Peasant Party politician whom King Peter had been pressed to accept for the sole purpose of getting rid of Mihailović and of reaching some settlement with Tito. The KPJ leadership should, however, beware of British duplicity.

It was then that the Germans surprised Tito at Drvar on 25 May as his staff, with attendant Allied missions and journalists, were about to celebrate his birthday. This well-planned airborne attack was part of another effort against the Yugoslav resistance, and aimed at seizing both Tito and Mihailović. Tito barely escaped capture, but lost touch with his forces, and the Russians, fearing for the co-ordinated control of his movement, pressed him to be evacuated to Italy. They eventually flew him out on 3 June, in one of their British-based transport planes from Bari.

Tito was then taken by the Royal Navy to the only Yugoslav island not to have been retaken by the Germans. More than 50 km. from the mainland, Vis had been turned into an Anglo-partisan base through which supplies reached the Communist movement. Massive support from the Western Allies saved the partisans, as the Soviets had saved their leader. Once again, a sharp turn was an excuse for Tito to leave a woman. Zdenka, who was showing signs of tuberculosis, was sent for treatment to the Soviet Union. In exchange, he was joined by Žarko, the son he had left in Russia, now a one-armed Red Army veteran who spoke only Russian.

Since Tito wanted political recognition from the Allies as a means of overcoming opposition at home, he was ready enough to pay for it by some tactical concessions to Šubašić, who was duly sent to Vis. The Tito-Šubašić agreement of 16 June 1944 was a breakthrough, but it was hardly a compromise. The leader of the People's Liberation Movement gave a formal assurance that the issue of the monarchy would not be raised while the war lasted, and stated that it was not his intention to impose Communism. The King's prime minister recognised the partisan-run 'people's' administration as the only authority on Yugoslav territory, and the NOV as the only legitimate fighting force. The task of his new and 'progressive' cabinet would be to organise outside support for the partisans.

He had yielded too much, and a worried Churchill took the opportunity of a visit to Italy in August to put the British idea of a compromise directly to Tito. The KPJ leader went reluctantly: he was flattered, but afraid of being tricked into a 'dark' British plan to restore the King or, at the very least, to preserve a chance for reactionaries to retrieve a share of power. His entourage even feared for his life. He went, determined to take all that the British would give, but to avoid any conditions.

General Maitland Wilson, the Allied commander in the Mediterranean theatre, believed that the Yugoslav partisans could shorten the war by crippling the Germans' retreat. Large quantities of arms were indeed sent from the summer onwards, but never enough for the recipients, who had their own ideas of how much they needed and deserved. It was difficult to convince Tito that the British were playing fair. He did assure Churchill that it was not his intention to impose Communism, but he would not endorse this publicly, nor would he meet the King.

He feared losing touch with developments in Yugoslavia if he stayed too long on Vis under British protection. His movement had hitherto fattened on the NDH. It had harnessed the plight of the western Serbs, then offered a way out to the increasing number of Croats who wanted to leave that sinking ship, and made the best of the failure of sectional nationalism. The situation was, however, different in eastern Yugoslavia, where the population was more homogeneous, was generally opposed to the Axis, had not turned against Yugoslavia, and stood behind Mihailović.

Serbia was once again a centre of attention. The Germans' principal line of retreat from the Balkans ran through it, and Djilas had passed on the Soviet message that it was the pivot on which turned the recognition of Tito's movement at the head of a greater South Slav state. He thus obtained full support from the Allies to build up the partisans' strength there.

Mihailović was stripped of his official position by the Šubašić government, and King Peter was made to appeal over the BBC on 12 September to all Yugoslavs to rally to Tito. The partisans were at last able to increase their following in Serbia again, but this was not done to the detriment of the Germans, who carried out an ordered evacuation over the summer as the best partisan units fought those of Mihailović. In July, Tito had asked Stalin to increase Soviet help, and even to intervene militarily in Serbia, in order to neutralise any covert Western plans. He eventually requested a meeting with Stalin, and (to use Churchill's expression) 'levanted' from Vis on 21 September. Unbeknownst to the British, the Soviets flew him out via their base in Bari and their headquarters in Romania.

He arrived in Moscow after an absence of five years, and came face to face with Stalin for the first time. As there is no other record of their talks but what Tito told Dedijer, we can only go by that and by what followed. They must have discussed international recognition for the People's Liberation Movement, how the Red Army would come to the partisans' help in Serbia, and their relations with Bulgaria. Stalin once again cautioned Tito against further antagonising the British.

The most important decision that they took was to disguise Tito's appeal for military intervention into a formal Soviet request to his National Committee for permission temporarily to enter Yugoslav territory bordering on Hungary. It was meant to say that no Western force would be able to land without similar consent, and amounted to a *de facto* recognition of his revolutionary administration. On 29 September, the British and US ambassadors were told of the agreement, which was also released to the media.

Tito obtained much more than he had hoped for. Stalin undertook to send a tank corps and to equip a dozen partisan divisions. Ever-increasing help followed, through bases in Romania. The details were worked out with Marshal Tolbukhin at his Romanian headquarters, where Tito stopped for more than a fortnight on his return. There he also met representatives of the Bulgarian Fatherland Front, to agree to Bulgarian troops turning from occupiers to liberators and fighting alongside his partisans in Yugoslavia. Only then did he return to his own NOV headquarters, back on the Yugoslav mainland, just across the Romanian border.

The Yugoslav Communist leaders were glad to have got rid of exclusive reliance on the British. On his way back from Moscow, Tito cabled an explanation of his sudden departure to the head of the British mission: reasons of state and strategy. He assured him that it signified no change of attitude, but rubbed in that 'we are an independent state, and I, as Chairman of the National Committee and Supreme Commander, am not responsible to anyone outside the country for my actions.'

Soviet troops helped the partisans to get through to Belgrade and, after a week-long battle with the retreating Germans, to install themselves in the capital. They also helped them to win Serbia from Mihailović. During most of that decisive October, Tito himself was not in Yugoslavia, and did not reach Belgrade until the 27th — a week after its liberation.

The behaviour of the Red Army did sometimes come as a surprise to the hero-worshipping partisans of the NOV, even if it duly impressed them by its might. By mid-November, it had gone on to Hungary, leaving the Yugoslavs to finish their own liberation and fight their civil war to an end. The Germans were eventually to capitulate in Yugoslavia on 15 May — seven months after the fall of Belgrade and more than a week after VE Day.

Although strengthened by Allied aid from both sides, by the Bulgarian army and by mass conscription in the now extended territories under its sway, the NOV found it difficult to switch to regular warfare in open country. As raw conscripts were hurled into a bloody war of attrition against a front that settled 100 km. west of Belgrade, but extended as far south as Sarajevo and to the sea, the Germans held their own until March 1945, and continued their orderly retreat through Montenegro and Bosnia.

The conquerors of Yugoslavia had not only destroyed the state in 1941, but set its components against each other. Yet the outcome of the Second World War led again led to a union, this time under Tito and the KPJ, as the defeat of the Axis destroyed those native movements that had withdrawn into the confines of sectional nationalism under foreign protection. The occupation had attempted to enforce a brutal order, mainly on the country's Serbian population, but without sufficient means — an ideal situation for the propagation of a revolutionary movement. Tito used the concept of 'national liberation' as an instrument of social upheaval and political conquest in the course of the many-faceted civil war that had raged under foreign rule.

Under Tito's direction, the KPJ had quickly established an

overall unity of strategy, which enabled it to exploit various situations and to practise different tactics while showing a single face to the outside world. This was in spite of the fact that some of the military aspects of Tito's leadership were dubious. As a general, he often could not see the wood for the trees, was ill-informed, gave contradictory orders, and made a series of glaring mistakes. But he would not be criticised.

Because he usually managed to recover his balance, his entourage looked up to him as an inspired strategist. He was an organiser and a political leader. He was not an adept of terror for its own sake, but he accepted it as an effective weapon if integrated in an overall plan.

Without contradiction or hypocrisy, he tied a popular resistance movement to the cause of world Communism led by the Soviet Union. In the course of the struggle against foreign occupation forces and native opponents, he forged a new power, and in so doing made little distinction between the revolutionary transformation of Yugoslavia and his own ascendancy over it.

4

FROM BALKAN STALIN TO
WOULD-BE WORLD LEADER, 1945–1960

Tito apes Stalin

The KPJ had had its unity tested during the war, but it had managed to organise the western Serbs' fight for survival while appealing to all those who opposed Serbia's real or apparent predominance in pre-war Yugoslavia, and then to offer Croats a way out of defeat while soothing Serbian sensitivities. The Party had squared it all within a different sort of Yugoslavia.

'Fraternity and unity' was Tito's own slogan, but it was hardly original, for he, like King Alexander, believed that the different nationalities would eventually blend into one nation. The federated units were not meant to be national units. Their borders were the result of bargaining within the leadership. Yugoslavia under Communist rule was politically, in spite of its federal appearance, at least as centralised as under the monarchy.

Tito had had to accept some transitory concessions of form to satisfy the Western Allies — a nominal regency and a provisional government in March 1945, under his premiership, to include a few of the London ministers. In this way, formal international recognition was given to the whole structure that had been set up by AVNOJ, under the control of the KPJ.

For the elections to the Constituent Assembly, a bogus Popular Front was set up. The campaign was organised as a plebiscite for Tito and the Front, and as a referendum against the King. Only the Front was able to present candidates; the Constituent Assembly was elected in November with a quasi-unanimity of votes, and proclaimed the Federal People's Republic of Yugoslavia by acclamation. It went on to adopt a Constitution on 31 January 1946, which sanctioned the country's new structure as a multinational federation of six republics: Slovenia, Croatia, Bosnia-Herzegovina, Serbia, Montenegro and Macedonia (with two

50

autonomous territories within Serbia — Voyvodina and Kosovo-Metohija, later to be called plain Kosovo).

Although the acknowledged master of the country, the 140,000-strong KPJ still hid behind the Front through which it wanted to mobilise the masses, and yet it no longer much cared for support as it eliminated a whole range of opponents, real or potential, imposing a repressive dogmatic regime through its control of the armed forces, the security services and the judiciary. The Central Committee elected in 1940 had never met as such, and all decisions were taken informally by its Politbureau. Tito, however, was clearly the boss, seconded by Kardelj, Ranković and Djilas, and cultivating a special relationship with the middle and lower Party cadres, who had come out of underground work and guerrilla warfare to take over the government and the economy, and were anxious to enjoy the fruits of victory.

Under his leadership, the new régime set out to emulate the Soviet model, much in advance of the other countries of eastern Europe. Its constitution was fashioned after Stalin's Soviet constitution of 1936, except that Tito was apprehensive about going quite as far with the right of self-determination. A formulation was devised to say that the peoples of Yugoslavia had already exercised it, by expressing their will to live together in the course of the partisan struggle. The Constitution made no mention of the KPJ, even though all power emanated from it, and its head was the real, but not the formal, head of the state, with a position and a cult that replicated Stalin's. Tito was 'the Marshal', with his unique uniform that would, in time, become ever more conspicuous, and already surrounded by a quasi-regal protocol.

He had immediately taken over the White Palace, the attractive country house in the semi-rural suburb of Dedinje that had been the residence of Prince Paul, but he was soon keeping it only as an official palace, preferring to live in a nearby villa that he would later expand into a vast compound. Various other abodes and hunting lodges were put at his disposal, so that by 1947 the prime minister's office already had twenty-five residences to look after.

He had never had much time for family relationships,[1] but when, after Zdenka's death in 1946, he finally moved to the house in Rumunska (later called Užička) street 15, the twenty-three-year-old NOV (perhaps secret police) Captain Jovanka Budisav-ljević was selected to be domestic superintendent there. A Serbian girl from Croatia whose family and village had been destroyed, she soon accompanied him on his visits abroad as personal secretary, but their liaison was kept secret.

Tito and the KPJ leadership also aped the Soviet economic model, introducing long-range planning in 1947 to create an industrial power from a nation of peasants. Relying on their help to repeat their achievements was but one of the misconceptions concerning what was expected of the Soviets, but never before 1948 was there any idea of deviating from what was understood to be Stalin's path. It was just that the Yugoslavs, having carried out their revolution, were full of dynamism.

No sooner had Tito been acknowledged as Yugoslavia's prime minister than he had gone straight back to Moscow, to sign in April 1945 with the Soviet Union a twenty-year treaty, considered the foundation-stone of his country's international position. On his return, he openly emphasised the Russian connection, expecting full Soviet economic and diplomatic support.

His foreign policy was expansionist from the start, and relations with the West deteriorated fast. He wanted to round off the South Slavs' ethnic domain at the expense of Italy and Austria, which were seen as defeated enemies, and he intended to force the decisions of the peace treaties, hence the race to Trieste that he ordered on his return from Moscow. When the peace conference on Italy opened in July 1946, he had again been to Moscow, where he had been showered with compliments. But however much Stalin might have liked Tito getting more territory to the west, he was not going to risk another war for that, and at the 1947 peace

---

[1]Zdenka, whom his entourage did not like, came back for a short while to the White Palace, as did Herta's five-year-old son Miša. With his elder son Žarko there was not much love lost. Tito's railwayman brother Martin, who lived in Hungary, did come and see him once in 1946, but on Tito's first return visit to his native village, no one knew him any longer.

treaties, Yugoslavia obtained no more than the Istrian peninsula.

Towards the south, the very concept of federation left Communist Yugoslavia open to new members. The link with Albania and Bulgaria had been envisaged by Tito as early as 1943, and talks had started behind closed doors with the leaders of the Communist parties of these two countries in the latter half of 1944. It was assumed that Yugoslavia's Kosovo region, with its large Albanian component, would become part of Albania, which would in turn become either the seventh unit of the Yugoslav federation, or a unit of the future Yugoslav-led Balkan federation, but Tito first had to restore Kosovo to Yugoslav rule. The establishment of a republic of Macedonia acknowledged that the region was one of ethnic transition between Serbs and Bulgars; it consolidated the KPJ's hold over a difficult region, and enabled it to look beyond, to the Bulgarian and Greek portions of Macedonia. Nevertheless, care had to be taken not to rush anything, in order not to provide ammunition to anti-Communist forces in all three countries or to the British.

Finally, the prospect was being opened to Tito's mind of being patron to a successful Communist revolution in Greece, so that by the end of 1947 his dream of a Balkan federation seemed to be moving towards reality. Nowhere else outside the Soviet Union was there yet a solid native leadership in command of the Party, administration, military and security; it was led by Tito, the first to have followed Stalin's example to be at once head of the Party, of the government and of the armed forces, as well as the source of ideological and cultural inspiration. He commanded the loyalty of the KPJ, and held undisputed sway over its organs of power.

As he had been calling for the re-establishment of the Comintern, only the Yugoslavs were decidedly enthusiastic when a new, somewhat subtler, agency was set up in September 1947 under the name of Information Bureau of Communist Parties (Cominform). They were given an important rôle in this new co-ordinating body of Europe's main Communist parties, which was a good camouflage for Soviet control, and one that would help to harness the Yugoslavs' proud dynamism to the collective aims of the Soviet camp that was being set up.

The clash with Stalin

Our perception of the break between Tito and Stalin has long been distorted by myths elaborated on both sides. It is now clear that it did not arise from any ideological difference, economic exploitation or nationalistic pride, but from power politics.

Tito regarded himself as the foremost representative of an expanding Communist world, not as the mere leader of a small country. The period 1945–7 was one when Communist parties were allowed to follow whatever path to power seemed best to each one of them, while the Soviet Union tried to get the most out of the postwar settlement and of instability in Western Europe. Stalin's strategy was not as monolithic as the West imagined, and it still allowed for differences of approach, within Communist parties and within his own Soviet party, which explains the encouragement given to Tito's radicalism by the Zhdanov faction of the Soviet leadership.

Stalin's strategy was then essentially defensive. Preoccupied with the security of the Soviet Union, he aimed at a protective glacis before risking revolution further away. Worried by Western perceptions of his policy, he would then move to check the radicals. The Yugoslav Communists did not understand this. Tito had total confidence in him. He accepted hierarchical authority in the Communist movement, but saw himself as being positioned just below Stalin, and believed that it was his duty to be both sword and shield to the movement.

He did in fact appear to be Number Two to Stalin, acting as protector to Balkan Communists, triumphantly received on his visits to east European capitals, proffering advice, criticism and help to various Communist parties. The superiority complex of Yugoslavia's rulers had certainly not endeared them to their opposite numbers in the neighbouring countries on the way to becoming 'people's democracies'.

The crisis in relations with Moscow arose out of Tito's ambitions outside Yugoslavia. It was difficult enough to keep any control over a Yugoslav Stalin, but this was nothing compared to the liability the Kremlin would have to face if a Balkan Stalin expected to share in the formulation of overall Communist-bloc policy, with naïve disregard for the realities of power at global level.

Stalin's fear was that Yugoslavia was beginning to see itself as a regional Communist centre, with all the possibilities of mischief in relation to the West, who viewed Tito as his Soviet master's catspaw. Yugoslav foreign policy was in Tito's hands, and it was getting into deep water. Because of increasing tension in Europe, the Soviets wished to prevent a situation likely to cause trouble in the Communist camp itself, and they wanted to be able to control Yugoslavia more directly in view of its important strategic position.

Stalin's attitude towards Yugoslavia's federal plans had oscillated for as long as these concerned the future. In January 1948, out of the blue, he asked for Djilas to come to Moscow to discuss various current issues, and Djilas later reflected that the Soviet dictator might have wanted to use him against Tito. Yugoslavia could swallow Albania — Stalin said. Negotiations on renewing the trade agreement dragged on, however. More Yugoslav delegates were then summoned, as well as Bulgarians. They were told to stop all further federation plans, and then to implement them forthwith, as the Yugoslavs in particular were rebuked for taking important foreign-policy decisions without closely consulting Moscow.

These were typical Stalinist moves, designed to test the Yugoslavs. In order to press home their intentions, the Soviets stepped up the pressure by withdrawing their advisers from Yugoslavia, and when Tito asked what it was all about, Molotov and Stalin wrote on behalf of the Soviet Party Central Committee on 27 March 1948, laying extraordinary ideological charges, and singling out for personal attack Tito's most trusted lieutenants, including Djilas.

'I felt as if a thunderbolt had struck me,' Tito told Dedijer,[2] and the thunderbolt forced the KPJ leadership out of its conspiratorial frame of mind. A letter written on behalf of the Soviet Central Committee needed a response from the Yugoslav Central

[2] *Tito Speaks*, London: Weidenfeld and Nicolson, 1953, p. 341.

Committee to give its leader legitimate support. As Tito penned a thirty-three-page draft answer, he consulted his closest advisers, who now met as a formal Politbureau (they were not quite certain who was actually part of that body), endorsed his initial reaction to reject the charges and blame them on misinformation, and decided to place it before the full Central Committee.

That plenary session, held behind closed doors on 12 April, was made all the more tense by the prospect of a new round of factional struggle within the KPJ; one member of the Central Committee, Andrija Hebrang, had just been removed as being an element of Soviet leverage. Tito's letter was endorsed, with the lone dissenting voice of Sreten Žujović, who was in turn removed.

Stalin had lost that first round, but he had circulated his letter to the other parties in the Cominform, with the request that they should express themselves on the subject. Their central committees hastened to comply, which hurt Tito, and Stalin wrote again to put the Yugoslavs firmly in their place, telling them that they had nothing so special to boast about, and that the issue would be formally put to the Cominform.

Invitations went out for a meeting to be held in Bucharest. The Yugoslav Central Committee met again several times in May, to expose publicly Hebrang and Žujović, to decide not to attend the Cominform session as the case against them had already been prejudged, and to convene a Party Congress. Stalin had done all he could to get the Yugoslav leaders to come, repeating the invitation, postponing the meeting, even appealing through the Poles.

In Bucharest on 28 June, the Cominform adopted a Resolution accusing the Yugoslavs of ideological deviations, and expelling them from the organisation. Tito, Kardelj, Djilas and Ranković were personally castigated, and 'healthy elements' within the KPJ were called on to overthrow their leadership. Nine months earlier, at the founding meeting, it had been the Yugoslavs themselves who had set a precedent to use the Cominform as a forum for operations against member-parties.

The Resolution brought the conflict into the open, and stunned the incredulous world. It was a typical Stalinist indictment, which revealed nothing of the real cause. Back in February a hint of things to come had been given with the removal of Tito's portraits in Romania, yet foreign diplomats in Moscow were surprised by the dramatic announcement, which came at a time when the Western press was reporting on Yugoslavia's military preparations against Italy. The vast majority of Yugoslavs could not believe their eyes.

The violence of the vocabulary was calculated to shock the Yugoslav leaders, and it did shock them, particularly Tito who, although he rarely departed from his regal calm, had been tense and nervous ever since the removal of his portraits in Bucharest, for he knew the meaning of Stalin's signals and pronouncements. He had been astonished by the brutality of the first letter, but when he received the text of the Resolution, he had his first and most violent attack of pain in the gall-bladder, which later required an operation.

At no time, however, did he hesitate. Stalin was confident that censure would be enough to bring the recusants back in line, or get them removed by their party. Beyond these expectations, he really had no plan. Tito immediately felt that his strength lay in the internationally recognised state that he ran through the KPJ, and on 29 June his Central Committee met again to reject and publish the charges.

For five months leading to that date, Tito had been trying to appease Stalin, whose charges were at best incidents inflated out of any inherent proportions, and at worst sheer nonsense. The correspondence, contemporary accounts and more recent findings do not give any basis for the theory of a rebellion by Tito against Stalin. The West did not realise that Tito's attempt to outdo Stalin had upset Stalin. It initially viewed the Soviet dictator's attempt to rein in the more reckless elements in his camp as another of his tricks to dupe his enemies, and then mistook it for a Yugoslav declaration of independence.

Stalinist resistance to Stalin

Tito had not wanted the clash. He and his ruling team instinctively clung to power, with a mixture of naïvety and shrewdness.

They realised that the slightest sign of weakness would have a negative effect on their followers, and Tito himself knew what awaited him if he gave in. In 1948, his fate was linked to his power, which he assimilated to the sovereignty of the state that he controlled. He told his entourage that these were the most terrible days of his life.

The clash happened at a time when the partisans' struggle was still a live force. The leadership was eventually able to capitalise on patriotism — the patriotism of the revolutionary war for the Communists and their sympathisers, and that of fear of the Russians among the population at large — but its immediate response was to maintain the momentum of its Stalinist programme in conditions of total isolation.

In the years following the war, Tito had taken the Party for granted, concentrating more on the repressive apparatus. Now he turned again to the KPJ. Stalin had berated him for not having held a congress since coming to power, and this was quickly put right, not only to show Stalin that the Yugoslav leadership was behaving correctly, but also to legitimise and reinforce Tito's position.

The Fifth Congress met in July to hear an eight-hour report by its secretary-general, and to re-elect a Central Committee. The report, on the achievements of the KPJ, was an indirect answer to Soviet accusations. The Central Committee was elected by secret ballot, from a list of names submitted to it. Messages of loyalty and love were addressed to Stalin, and Tito rounded off the proceedings with the cry 'Long live the Soviet Union! Long Live Comrade Stalin!'

Rather like the Catholic faithful of England in 1535, the Communists of Yugoslavia did not really know what it was all about. There was widespread belief that it would all be overcome, but the 'healthy elements' to whom the Resolution had appealed existed in no small numbers. Ivo Banac, their most recent historian, estimates them to have been at least 11 per cent of the membership, and perhaps as much as one-fifth. They tended to come from the élite, from all factions, regions and institutions, but they were too scattered in motivation to develop a single movement, especially once the steamroller of secret-police repression got moving to crush them.

As the number of political trials increased, the security services attended to Communist as well as to non-Communist subversiveness. Terror ensured an all-risks guarantee of loyalty within the KPJ. Tito personally ordered the arrest of the more important, and took the decision to send 'Cominformists' to special camps before these had even been organised, let alone legalised.[3] Cominformism, like collaborationism before it, was an opportunity to get rid of potential trouble-makers. The losers of the old factions who had survived previous purges were now swept away.

Tito fought back by adopting an even harsher Stalinist line, by expropriating what little remained of 'capitalism', by accelerating the collectivisation of agriculture, and by strengthening the Party and the security apparatus. The repression intensified the dictatorship, and increased the prestige of Ranković's police. The rôle of the Party was extended because it was the only source of legitimacy once that obtained from Moscow had been removed, and because its cadres linked their fate to Tito's towering authority. If the personality cult appeared to have lessened somewhat after the clash, the gradual removal of Stalin as a transcendental inspirer, and the need to have a symbol larger than the Party, soon built it up again.

Initially nothing changed in the relations between the Soviet and Yugoslav governments, both sides treating the issue as being strictly between their respective parties. Yugoslavia put on a show of politeness for the Danube Conference — the first international gathering to be held in post-war Belgrade — and toed the Soviet line, as it would do at other such meetings, but Tito himself carefully stayed away.

The Soviets first attacked by proxy, through other Communist parties, manipulated tensions between Yugoslavia and its

---

[3] Two barren uninhabited islands in the Adriatic were selected to be this Yugoslav *gulag*, where some 15,000 KPJ members were sent without trial to be 're-educated' under torture, and to do aimless, 'socially useful' hard labour, under a system run by prisoners who had repented of their offences.

neighbours, and made use of every vulnerable point, regardless of contradictions and falsehoods. From attacks on Tito the nationalist, which had strengthened him among the population at large more than it had weakened him among Communists, the propaganda campaign changed to saying that he had moved into the imperialist camp. At the same time, the liquidation of alleged 'Titoists' in the satellite states conveniently labelled leaders whom Stalin wanted to get rid of as he was consolidating the Soviet camp; it had nothing to do with Tito.

Yugoslavia's isolation was complete, and yet, although Tito remained anxious for another year and a half to avoid conflict with the Soviet Union, and to have as little to do with the West as possible, there is evidence that he suspected the Americans would not allow the Soviets actually to intervene by force of arms. From regarding Yugoslavia as the Kremlin's spearhead, the West turned to assuming that the break had resulted from a conscious decision by Tito to stand up to Stalin rather than from a defensive reaction.

For fear of an economic collapse creating a power vacuum, which would be filled by a régime completely subservient to Moscow, it was decided in the autumn of 1948 (in the words of Ernest Bevin, the British Foreign Secretary) to keep Tito afloat. By the following spring, 'Titoism' was being used to denote a form of Communism seeking to be independent of the Soviet Union, and the West moved to a policy designed to encourage the satellites to follow Tito's example. His régime was seen as a wedge which could break up the Communist monolith, and it would thus be helped to remain in power through aid given without political strings — although there was linkage with the end of its involvement in the Greek civil war. This would then evolve into the view that Tito would offer a liberalised version of Communism, but its premise was that he was useful to the West.[4]

---

[4] It was a British idea to help Tito's régime survive, as proof that it was possible for a Communist government to exist without Soviet support, and it was taken up by the United States in order to exploit the split as a potential advantage in the Cold War. The French, who had less influence, remained generally sceptical of Anglo-Saxon hopes regarding the effect that the Yugoslav case might have on the satellites.

An important part in this scenario was played by all those who, in the West and more particularly in Britain, had accepted and built up Tito as the progressive and patriotic hero of the Second World War who had united his compatriots in the fight against Nazi-fascism. They were back on stage again after a small interval to present him, according to their different convictions, as a worthy friend of Britain or as the embodiment of progressive, non-Stalinist Communism, and they would continue to do so until the very end.

The zigzags of change

By 1950 Stalin had tried everything short of war to overthrow Tito, but that last option had become too dangerous. The Yugoslav example had failed to attract imitators, but in the wake of the Korean War, the Western powers were keen to draw Tito's country into their camp, with the British in particular entertaining hopes for the liberalisation of his régime.[5] Eventually, but not before 1953, and only for a very brief period, he did reluctantly establish a link with the Western alliance through a treaty with Greece and Turkey — the Balkan Pact.

Western help enabled Yugoslavia to withstand Soviet pressure, and its leadership to move on to expressing the conflict in ideological terms. It was in 1950 that the régime began a gradual shift of emphasis from intimidation to persuasion. Djilas was the driving force behind a new line intent on showing that, whereas Marxism had reached a dead end in the Soviet Union, it was moving ahead in Yugoslavia. It was not easy to sell to Tito Djilas's idea of 'self-management' — of factories and other economic concerns being run by workers' delegates. Tito eventually came to accept it as a good way of sounding more Communist than the

[5] Tito had been fully re-glamorised with the British public through the medium of war-time connections. An echo of this now largely forgotten admiration could be heard many years later, when the actor Timothy West told George Greig of *The Sunday Times* that Tito had been his hero in his student days at the Regent Street Polytechnic in the early 1950s (*NatWest Dimensions — The Magazine for Decision Makers*, Summer 1989, p. 28).

Soviet Union, yet more democratic than the West, and himself introduced the necessary legislation in June. This was the first step in the setting up of institutions aimed at giving those people integrated in the system the feeling of participation in the day-to-day decision-making process at the local level.

It was easier to get Tito to take to the idea of a change of name for the KPJ — to League of Communists of Yugoslavia (SKJ) — to symbolise its new rôle as more of an ideological consciousness-raiser than a power transmission-belt. This was done at its Sixth Congress, staged in November 1952 as an anti-Stalinist demonstration and as a solemnisation of the move to a higher phase of Marxism. A new Constitutional Law followed in January 1953, to enshrine the concept of socialist direct democracy as the expression of the working people through self-management. It introduced the office of president of the Republic, head of state, government and army, to which Tito would duly be elected after the general elections held at the end of that year.

When Tito even assented to put an end to the disastrous collectivisation of agriculture, genuine hopes for more real change were aroused — until Stalin's death on 5 March 1953. The storm over the Trieste issue with Italy that followed in the autumn of that year was meant to stress Yugoslavia's independence from the West at a time when changes could be sensed in the Soviet Union, before Tito agreed a year later to a settlement of that vexed question along the lines suggested by the West. The final obstacle to Yugoslavia's incorporation into the Western defence system had been removed, but Tito was no longer interested.

Within a year of Stalin's death, the Balkan Pact was a dead letter, and Yugoslav foreign policy a blend of Tito's longing for a bigger rôle, Communist ideology, and the traditional balance resulting from his country's unchanged geopolitical position. As blocs hardened, non-alignment was in the air, particularly in Asia and Africa, and Tito was quick to see its possibilities. By associating with the Third World, he could play down his dependence on the West, look forward to a reconciliation with the Soviet Union, and satisfy his ambition by bidding for leadership of the non-aligned. On returning from an eight-month tour of Asia, he gave speeches in February 1955 condemning the division of the world into two antagonistic blocs, and praising the peaceful nations in between (including his own) who worked for the elimination of the blocs.

He had also worked hard on improving relations with the new Soviet leaders, and the well-prepared visit in May of Bulganin and Khrushchev, however strained, formalised the reconciliation. The 1955 Belgrade Declaration that he signed with Bulganin on behalf of the two governments amounted to a real treaty of friendship. The Twentieth Congress of the Soviet Communist Party in February 1956, followed by the dissolution of the Cominform in April, permitted Tito to think that Titoism had triumphed over Stalinism.

His return visit to the Soviet leaders in June was a warm display of friendship renewed. This time, the two ruling parties' ideological alliance was clearly sealed in another joint declaration. 'In time of war as in time of peace', Tito said in a speech, 'Yugoslavia marches shoulder-to-shoulder with the Soviet people towards the same goal — the victory of socialism.'

Khrushchev was ready to acknowledge the Yugoslavs' right to their own socialist ways, in return for help in dealing with the growing unrest in the satellites, and Tito was willing to help, in return for Khrushchev's recognition of him as friend and partner. Both were anxious that the de-Stalinisation process should be an ordered one, but Tito did not want to be trapped into renewed subordination to Moscow. It was a reconciliation, but one that would be difficult to consummate.

That summer and autumn they were in close contact, coming and going unexpectedly on private visits. Consulted on questions that did not directly concern Soviet-Yugoslav relations, Tito must have thought that he stood a fair chance of realising his ambition of influencing the Communist régimes of Eastern Europe. When the Hungarian revolution broke out in November, Khrushchev flew in to consult him on the eve of the Soviet armed intervention, to which the Yugoslav leader readily gave his assent, but the mutual goodwill was soon dispelled by the execution of Imre Nagy, the revolutionary government's prime minister who had sought refuge in the Yugoslav embassy. Tito felt double-crossed and compromised. His position appeared so contradictory that he had to give a public explanation: Soviet intervention was a lesser evil than counter-revolution.

Relations were strained again, but the two men had sympathy for, and faith in, each other, which helped them to gloss over difficulties at a time when they were anxious to go on working together. Khrushchev was preparing a gathering of Communist parties in Moscow for the fortieth anniversary of the Revolution, to confirm the leadership of the Soviet Union, and Tito was planning a new congress of his SKJ, as Yugoslavia's bid to participate in that leadership. They met again, and Tito promised to attend the Moscow meeting.

The fortieth anniversary was not the consummation of full reconciliation. The draft declaration to be put to the ruling parties made Tito fear that the meeting would be used to press him back into the flock. He pleaded ill-health to avoid going to Moscow, and the SKJ did not subscribe to the document of the ruling parties, although it did to the manifesto of all the sixty-eight parties which endorsed the Soviet Union's foreign-policy position. The draft programme to be put to Tito's Seventh Congress in 1958 then sounded to the Russians too much like a manifesto of polycentrism, and they, along with most sister-parties, decided that they would not go to Belgrade. The attempt to close the gap between Tito's and Khrushchev's conceptions of the reorganisation of the Communist world had failed. In view of the growing difficulties in Sino-Soviet relations, Tito could nevertheless still hope for the day when the Soviet leadership would once again call for his help.

His active involvement with the Third World increased in consequence, as he needed to promote his image as a leader of world opinion outside the two blocs. Between the end of 1958 and the beginning of 1961, he made more extended tours of Asia and Africa, and dramatically took the lead of the non-aligned at the 1960 session of the UN General Assembly. His efforts culminated in the Conference of Heads of State and Government of Non-Aligned Countries held in Belgrade in September 1961, testifying to the prestige that his activities had earned him. The participants had been selected on the criterion of their none-too-favourable feelings for the West. Tito's successful cultivation of them provided him with a platform from which he could offer help to Moscow, while he continued to try and induce the Soviet leadership to correct its mistakes for the good of worldwide Communism.

Reconciliation with the Soviet Union had also been necessary to end the confusion that had spread to his own SKJ, where Djilas had taken to applying the criticism of Soviet reality to Yugoslav reality. In January 1954, Tito stepped in and manoeuvred the Central Committee to exclude him for his ideological deviations. Djilas's disgrace, followed by his three trials in 1955–7, and his subsequent incarceration (1956–61, 1962–6), symbolised the end of liberalisation. Although there was to be no return to the draconian methods of the post-war years, Tito's régime kept to the narrower path of monopolistic Communism at home, while it trod the broad way of multifarious socialism in the world at large.

Convinced that the long-term success of the revolution called for a strong leader no less than a strong Party, he favoured his own cult. Dedijer's 'His Master's Voice' biography, *Tito Speaks*, was serialised and published throughout the world, while volume after volume of Tito's collected (and re-written) speeches and articles was added to all the public libraries in Yugoslavia. Life at what his entourage commonly called 'Court' was becoming more and more regal and luxurious. The state visits to Turkey and Greece in 1954 had led to a great increase in the formality of protocol. In the winter, Tito often spent time in the sixteenth-century castle of Brdo in Slovenia, which had been used by Prince Paul before the war, but his favourite residence was soon the Brioni archipelago off the Istrian coast on which no expense was spared.[6]

[6] Tito chose Brioni on account of its specially healthy climate. It had been used as a summer retreat by high society since Roman days, and was taken over for Tito's exclusive use in 1949. His numerous residences were embellished with works of art taken from museums, or provided by his friend Ante Topić-Mimara. The latter, a mysterious character who had been commissioned to obtain restitution to Yugoslavia of works of art taken by the Nazis, amassed a great, heterogeneous and somewhat doubtful collection, which he left to the city of Zagreb when he died in 1987.

He held to the basic tenets of Marxism, of which he had but superficial knowledge. Ideology for him was inseparable from politics, and he was suspicious of new ideas, even if he came to adopt them for public relations purposes. Although he had no interest in anything that could be called cultural, he nevertheless had a soft spot for writers and artists, who contributed to his prestige and that of the Yugoslav revolution. His Serbo-Croat, evolved from the speech of his native Zagorje, and influenced by his mother's Slovene, as well as by long spells among speakers of German and Russian, was so difficult to locate that many people thought he could not be a native Yugoslav. He had acquired fluent German and Russian, and was intent on learning English too. Sociable and hospitable, he had always been keen on comfort, and was now keen on respectability too.

Having ordered those of his entourage who had failed to observe such proprieties to enter into matrimony ('*Chez vous, les noces se succèdent,*' observed the French ambassador's wife), he too formally married Jovanka Budisavljević at the beginning of 1952,[7] and thereafter cast her in the public rôle of First Lady corresponding to his conception of his own prestige.

---

[7]'He was young for his years and had remarkable physical vitality,' wrote Phyllis Auty admiringly, 'so that the discrepancy in years — not so unusual among the South Slavs as it is in Western Europe — appeared to be of little importance.' (*Tito: A Biography*, London: Longman, 1970, p. 288.)

5

THE LAST DECADES, 1961–1980: HELMSMAN AND PHARAOH

The reform waves

Yugoslavia had eventually achieved her industrial take-off, but only with massive aid from the West, and at the expense of food production and economic efficiency. Self-management had had no more economic foundation than the centralised command economy. The 1960s would be characterised by a continuous tug of war between 'reformists', striving for more economic efficiency, and 'conservatives', defending the SKJ's power basis. The decade started off in 1961 with an experiment in economic reform which never dared go very far, as Tito ushered in a campaign against liberal trends the following year.

Then in April 1963, a third Constitution was enacted which introduced at last a real measure of decentralisation, with one of the most complicated political systems in existence, and the SKJ enshrined as the motive force of society. The state became the Socialist Federal Republic of Yugoslavia. Personnel rotation was introduced for all elective functions, except for the yet further elevated presidency. Tito effectively became life president, as the Constitution stated that no limitations of office applied to him.

He now enjoyed quasi-monarchical attributes. Stamps and gold coins bore his portrait. Because of his ever more exalted status, the increasing complexities of affairs of state, and his age too, he began to withdraw from the day-to-day running of business, while keeping foreign policy and the prestige of Communist Yugoslavia as his personal prerogative. Kardelj, the theoretician in charge of ideology and planning, and Ranković, the watchdog in charge of security and organisation, were still at his side, but a secret struggle for the succession had already begun between them.

The Sino-Soviet dispute gave Tito his chance to move closer to

67

Khrushchev again in 1962, as he tightened the reins at home. Before the end of that year, there had been an exchange of visits, with Tito being granted the privilege of addressing the Supreme Soviet. On returning home, he felt able to confirm the identity of aims of Yugoslavia and the Soviet Union. Relations were further intensified with another exchange of visits in 1963, before Khrushchev was forced to step down in 1964. Tito was initially dispirited by this turn of events, but he was reassured as it became clear that Brezhnev and Kosygin were not going to change their predecessor's policy towards Yugoslavia, and he was soon busy again offering his services.

Non-alignment nevertheless remained the established basis of Yugoslavia's foreign policy. Tito felt no inconsistency in wanting equality between all (or at least all important) Communist parties, on the one hand, and a strong Communist community (with the Soviet Union), on the other. He also saw no inconsistency in wanting to play a major role in that Communist community, and to lead the Third World. He hoped to influence the evolution of Communist régimes, and considered himself to be the best propagator of socialism among the under-developed.

Meanwhile, the half-hearted experiment with economic reform had ground to a halt. Inflation and foreign debt had grown to a point where it was feared that Western aid would stop unless there was a return to economic reform. Backed by another assistance package, the 1965 reforms did at last break the back of centralised state control over the economy, and led to the fall of Ranković, who was made the scapegoat for all previous failures.

The Constitution of 1963 encouraged a closer association between nationality and territory, at a time when the political élite was concerned to find some solution which would allow it to meet the challenges of a new epoch, and retain power without returning to authoritarian centralisation. Unable to satisfy the up-and-coming generation with real economic enterprise, let alone with more political freedom, the régime was turning a blind eye to sectional national differences infiltrating the power structure. It had actively discouraged all integrative forces other than

Communism, and separate nationalisms were surfacing again with decentralisation.

All this had not been to the liking of Ranković, who had opposed the accelerated pace of change, and who had thus become the standard-bearer of those who impeded economic reform. In the spring of 1966, a plot was hatched against him with Tito's approval, in which he was accused, among other things, of planting listening devices in the President's own residence. Isolated and humiliated, he resigned from all his functions, but was not prosecuted. He remained loyally silent until his death in 1983. Tito had shown that his manipulative powers were as strong as ever. He immediately went on to warn all those who, at home and abroad, longed for a Yugoslavia that would no longer be socialist that the SKJ would be kept strong and disciplined until the Yugoslavs' Communist consciousness had developed to the point where the guiding force of the Party would no longer be necessary.

A new lease of hope was given to reform, but what happened fell short of expectations. Yugoslavia became an open country where travel was concerned, for her citizens were allowed to emigrate in search of employment abroad. For the rest, the economy was simply turned over to the partial control of the republican bureaucracies. Regional economic and political rivals would turn for support to local feelings of identity, and nationality would cause divisions within the SKJ cutting across those between reformists and conservatives. Of the original set of Tito's lieutenants only Kardelj remained, less of an heir-apparent groomed for the succession than an heir-presumptive who could be trusted to superintend a smooth transition.

A strange period ensued. The process of transforming the state structure went on in a fairly tumultuous fashion. Republican leaderships increasingly implemented their own policies within their territories, sometimes boosted by (and boosting) traditional national ideologies, and helped by artificial economic growth, duplication of structures and inefficiently utilised credits.

Tito busied himself again with world affairs. A further exchange of visits with Brezhnev had fully reaffirmed Yugoslavia's special relations with the Soviet Union when, as a result of events in the eastern Mediterranean in 1967 (the Greek Colonels' coup and the Israeli victory over three Arab states in the Six-Day War), the tone of his pronouncements that summer became openly anti-Western. He fully aligned himself with Moscow, because he was no neutral in the Near East. The Arab cause had been one of the vehicles for his promotion of socialism around the Mediterranean. Nasser's defeat had come as a blow, and he feared that if the Egyptian leader were to fall in consequence of it, Yugoslavia's influence in the Arab world would be greatly reduced. He further saw in Israel's victory the beginnings of American action to alter the balance of power in the area, and a threat to Communist Yugoslavia.

The Soviet government, however, was not particularly anxious for confrontation with the United States, and there was a noticeable lack of ardour in the SKJ for Tito's truculent rhetoric against Israel and Western imperialism in the name of socialism and non-alignment. More realistic counsels eventually prevailed, and Tito changed his tune from *revanche* to mediation — which could also satisfy his pride. He turned to mobilising world opinion to restore, as much as possible, the situation that preceded the Six-Day War.

Yugoslavia's international rôle had brought the country a measure of independence and much glamour. Tito's prestige in Asia and Africa was one of the reasons for the attention paid to him by the Soviet Union. In the 1960s, Yugoslav foreign policy was occasionally as close to the Soviet as that of any Warsaw Pact ally — when their interests coincided. Tito longed for such situations. He was overjoyed when he was again showered with honours in Moscow in 1967 on the fiftieth anniversary of the Revolution. He altered his own texts for a new edition of his complete works to remove criticism of the Soviet Union, and even talked of a similarly expurgated new edition of *Tito Speaks*.

When the Soviet Union resorted to pressure, however, he resisted, and made sure that the world knew about it, always conveying to the West in particular his anxieties about such pressure, and his willingness to resist it, provided that the requisite degree of backing was forthcoming. Once this had been obtained, he was quick to stress how good Soviet-Yugoslav relations were.

Yugoslavia did not associate itself with preparations for the meeting of Communist parties planned for the autumn of 1968, and in April, on his return from yet another Asian tour, Tito went to Moscow to make his position clear. He was worried about the negative influence that a Soviet naval presence in the Mediterranean, and pressure of the Soviet Union's European allies, might have on the Communist community. He was now working on a third non-aligned summit, and was also paying more attention to Europe again, going as far as to curry favour with General de Gaulle, whom he had come to see as a Western counterpart to himself.

The Great Fear of 1968 and after

Ideology had come to occupy the top place in Yugoslavia's non-alignment. Its defence plans envisaged action against NATO only, when its vital interests appeared to be placed in jeopardy by the 1968 Warsaw Pact invasion of Czechoslovakia. It had supported the reform movement in that country, because Tito believed this to be in the best interests of socialism, but he had taken care to advise the Communist leadership in Prague on how far it could safely go. When he went there ten days before the invasion, far from offering moral support against the Soviet Union, he spoke of the dangers of reaction, counter-revolution and Western imperialism. He wanted to believe that a solution had been found.

The Kremlin's military intervention in Czechoslovakia thus strained his faith in the Soviet Union and worsened relations once again. Tito condemned it as a serious blow against socialism (this time, there was no talk of a lesser evil) and expressed his country's determination to defend its independence, taking a joint stand with Romania's Communist leader Ceauşescu to resist aggression.

With the formulation of the 'Brezhnev doctrine' of the limited sovereignty of socialist states, he looked anew to the West for serious cover, but immediately rejected the US idea of a 'grey zone', including Yugoslavia, to be shielded by NATO, saying that since nothing had changed in his country, he had no reason to believe that the Soviet Union would attack it. It soon appeared, as before, that both sides were anxious to avoid a breach. To check the advance of non-Communist influences at home, Tito hastened to restore working relations with the Soviets. By August 1969, he was able to state that mutual efforts were well on the way to eliminating the consequences of the 'events of August last year'.

Plans for another conference of the non-aligned had naturally been interrupted by these 'events', but Tito was intent on reviving them, however difficult the task might be. By then, there were almost as many definitions of non-alignment as there were non-aligned governments, but it remained the only foreign policy acceptable to all trends of the SKJ, and Tito was wedded to it. So, at the age of seventy-seven, he went off personally to canvass African leaders, and the Third Conference duly met in Lusaka in September 1970, with Tito occupying a place of honour next to the host, President Kaunda.

He nevertheless realised that the influence of the movement was declining, and was anxious not to appear to be forgetting the West, the European Economic Community in particular. On his return from Lusaka, he travelled to five EEC countries, but not before he had received President Nixon. By the end of the 1960s, Yugoslavia's foreign policy was a compound of megalomaniac tendencies, ideological inclinations, political necessities, economic realities and reflexes of fear, but it was definitely Tito's.

If life in Yugoslavia had generally improved, it was certainly not due to economic efficiency. In the absence of a realistic and open discussion of the issues available, the changes brought about by modernisation were taking place, not only in a very bad economic climate, but also in an ever more fragmented social system.

On the problems of economic reforms, constitutional arrangements and national identity, the SKJ was so divided that it was no longer clear what it was trying to do. Authority was being challenged by local Communist groups and ethnic feelings, by churches and intellectuals, by workers and students, as well as by general hooliganism and rampant corruption. The ideology of the ruling élite no longer satisfied even its own children.

A threshold had been reached in the late 1960s, in politics, in economics and in society, which would require a redistribution of power. How much, in what way, and by what criteria this would come about had become a matter of debate. The confused and heterogeneous awakening introduced by the reformist waves culminated in 1968. The Belgrade students' revolt in June of that year, coming after the Prague Spring, and followed by mass demonstrations of the Kosovo Albanians in November in favour of an upgrading of their region to republican status, presented the Party apparatus with its most serious challenge since it had come to power. It showed too that people at the top were still united by the simple reflex of preserving their power, as theirs was the organisation and the ability to manoeuvre within and around the disorganised and unco-ordinated opposition trends. When the students demanded social justice, Tito appeared on television. He pledged himself to solve their problems, appealed to them to help him root out opposition to reform, and warned them to beware of infiltration by 'hostile elements'. He then went on to take a similar line with the workers.

The government had managed to turn the explosion of disaffection among workers and students into a movement of support for Tito's 'revolutionary' leadership. Fear of the Russians did the rest. A series of stop-gap measures blending concessions and threats managed to restore a modicum of calm. Once the great fear of 1968 had been overcome, with a sense of having Western support against the Soviet threat, a fragile unity of Party line and public opinion was achieved again. A Ninth SKJ Congress was held in March 1969, to restore the balance between economic reform and Party authority. Tito's opening speech set the tone, by insisting on the continued revolutionary nature of the SKJ: liberalisation had gone too far; there was to be strong leadership; new blood would be brought in.

The Ninth Congress both backpedalled on democratisation, and shifted power to the republics. The new line could be described as a counter-reform, at the same time anti-democratic and confederalist. The Communist organisation of Croatia had been going its own way, espousing what soon became the 'mass movement' of Croatian resentment at the end of 1971. The fear of a ground swell, coinciding with external events, brought the central leadership to react with Tito's full authority in 1971–2.

After a general tightening up on the ideological, cultural and educational front, a purge of the technocratic élites, a limitation of basic civil rights, and the restoration of full political control over press and publishing, new constitutional amendments in June 1971 re-defined the state as very close to a confederal union. This was followed by a thorough cleansing from the political apparatus of all those who, in the republics, had begun to assert their authority, and had acquired a genuine audience. They were accused of nationalism, liberalism and technocratism, the emphasis varying according to location — more particularly nationalist tendencies in Croatia, and liberal tendencies in Serbia. The purge went on right through 1972.

The replacements were more subservient and less competent protégés of the old guard. Tito's new trusties in the republics and provinces were grey men. Power was shared out, or 'feudalised' (to use Djilas's description), in exchange for adherence to a strict Party line. Heads had rolled (metaphorically) in the regions, and had been replaced by promotions from the middle cadres who, as ever, understood what Tito was trying to say and do. As in all crises, he had turned to them, and now rewarded them with territorial power.

He wanted to ensure that power remained in the SKJ, with no further watering down of Communist ideology. He had called a halt to further change, and returned to the formulas of his younger days — Party, class struggle, democratic centralism, the enemy. The reforms came to an end, except for the continued implementation of greater autonomy for the six republics and for Serbia's two associated provinces, as a counterpart to reinforced Party unity.

Tito appeared as the sheet-anchor in a storm of change. At home, he was supreme arbiter between different trends, and foreign policy was entirely his own. At the Eighth Congress, in 1964, his Party title had been changed from secretary-general to president of the League. At the Ninth Congress, in 1969, speakers referred to 'Tito's epoch'. His personal involvement in all fields greatly increased again. At the age of seventy-nine, he gathered all his energy to hold the system together, to act the parts of inspirer, helmsman, father and commander.

He went on extensive visitations around the country, to put across the newly-hardened line, and in 1970 he was globe-trotting again. More than ever before, the régime and the country were linked to his person. The expression 'Tito's Yugoslavia' was in increasing use. New biographies glorified his legend for home and foreign consumption.[1] Schoolchildren learned his life and achievements by rote, and confectioners sold cakes in the shape of his head.

Ever watchful of the prestige of Communist Yugoslavia, Tito carefully checked the design of all symbols and uniforms, while his own uniforms, in seasonal versions and in various colours, with matching shoes, resplendent with gold braid and decorations, were balanced against hardly less showy civilian outfits for every possible occasion. His long foreign tours, particularly when he went by sea aboard his yacht in the early 1960s before he took to air travel, were spectacular, with naval and air escorts, a numerous suite in attendance, and a fleet of cars, bands and communication links. Protocol became more elaborate, with rules of dress and address, and gun salutes.

Wherever he turned up in Yugoslavia, troops, police, security services, local authorities, republican grandees, workers and schoolchildren turned up for bigger and bigger welcoming ceremonies. He thoroughly enjoyed it all, and organised fantastic hunts and great banquets for hundreds of guests. His jubilees and other celebrations linked to his person were ritualised. A special museum was built in the grounds of his Belgrade residence to house the gifts he had received, and a private zoo was set up on Brioni for the animals he had been given.

In this court life his wife Jovanka Broz (the additional surname Tito he shared with neither sons nor wife) took an increasing rôle. Not only did she, naturally enough, accompany him on his tours

---

[1] Vinko Vinterhalter's *Zivotnom stazom Josipa Broza* (Belgrade, 1968; English-language edn, *In the Path of Tito*, 1972) and Phyllis Auty's *Tito: A Biography* (London, 1970).

and visits, but she took part in SKJ congresses. She now had her say in appointments to the President's office and household, often attended informal consultations between the President and his advisers, and on Tito's orders was even given ambassadors' dispatches to read. She is said to have influenced honours and promotions. Tito's entourage did not like her, nor did his sons,[2] and she was never popular.

Tito had never been a recluse, and he had not neglected contact with the people, but towards the end of the 1960s, dazzled as he was by the idolatry of which he was the object, his sense of realities had probably been dulled, and his self-criticism certainly weakened. His political realism and adaptability notwithstanding, his mentality had become that of an old revolutionary turned conservative. The dogmatic tone of his pronouncements on everything under the sun, ranging from American foreign policy to the cinema, from Marx to cattle-breeding, had an increasingly anachronistic ring. He had never been a great public speaker; his rhetoric was now empty.

Orthodox but feudal

Tito's rule was autocratic rather than totalitarian. He was intent on controlling the immediate sources of power — the Party, the armed forces and the security services. The rest concerned him less, so that the economy or culture could enjoy some autonomy, so long as changes in these fields did not threaten the continuity of political power, or, better still, in so far as they contributed to that continuity. By the late 1960s, such changes had reached the point where it was feared that they would destroy the régime, and Tito had acted dazzlingly to maintain the foundations of Communism as he knew them.

Order had been restored, but at a price. The purges had been carried out by relying on alliances with and within the various local leaderships, and they had left the SKJ shorn of many of its

---

[2] Their own relations with Tito were not all that harmonious, although in the 1960s they came for a family lunch on their father's birthday.

prominent personalities, thus precipitating the decline in the prestige of the ruling Party. Tito had also pointed to the army as the bastion not only of the country's independence but of its social and political order as well, and thus turned it into something of an extended praetorian guard. The stress on the army symbolised the power of the state behind the historic leader, as the Party was being revitalised.

Tito had endorsed the concept of self-management as a public-relations exercise to rehabilitate Yugoslavia in the 'socialist' move-ment. After going through various hesitant phases, it ended up as a consolidated and all-embracing ideology, with which the SKJ, duly purged, could hold the country together. Self-management was supposed to be the extension to every institution in the land (save the military) of the initial idea of management of factories by workers' delegates. In theory, it was a form of direct demo-cracy, but in practice it was a combination of decentralisation without democratisation and of patronage politics. As credit and investment decisions were left to the republics, regional govern-ments used their powers to maximise the amount of resources to satisfy their own bases.

Massive government intervention in the economy started again, at regional level. Inefficiencies and structural imbalances increased as each republic strove after self-sufficiency. In effect, there was re-centralisation into eight centres, with eight little Party-state economies together producing more than they earned, leading to enormous foreign debt, rising inflation and unemployment.

With a balance-of-payments deficit of $3,400 million in 1979, Tito upheld his country as a model to no less a forum than the Assembly of the International Monetary Fund meeting in Belgrade. Deficit and debt for the insufficiently developed — he argued — assured equality between regions, whatever the degree of development; the world economy should be balanced in the way that the Yugoslav economy was balanced.

As cultural isolationism followed economic isolationism down the path which led to identifying republics with ethnic groups, Serbian nationalism reacted against a trend which left over 40 per cent of Serbs outside Serbia. The fact that the apparatus of the largest republic had done less than the others to tap such feelings increased the malaise of Serbs who, in the 1960s, had already begun to ponder seriously the consequences of their dispersal.

No longer independent of regional leaderships, who controlled the appointment, or rather the delegation, of personnel to all central institutions, the federal government was nevertheless still a powerful broker. Its ability to work out compromises, backed when necessary by Tito's power to knock republican heads together, remained a major factor in the successful avoidance of inter-regional deadlocks. The President's personal authority to intervene in any matter did counter-balance the feudalisation of the power apparatus, but his arbitrations could be no more than palliatives.

A genuine democracy and a genuine market could have given Yugoslavia a chance to find real foundations, but Tito had in the 1960s opposed the granting of freedoms which would have led to the end of the system he had come to personify. All that the leadership could resort to in the 1970s was the 'agreed economy', the SKJ and . . . Tito. What had come to be called the agreed economy was the way in which political pressures were applied to what market forces had been released so as to produce the 'right' decisions.

The SKJ did reconsolidate itself ideologically, and its leadership did hold together under Tito, but the eight locally-based Communist hierarchies would thereafter resist any attempt at reintegration, either from above (through a reinforcement of federal decision-making) or from below (through the autonomous forces of civil society). Even Tito was no longer able to oppose disintegration, for it would have meant provoking a new crisis, with uncertain results. 'Yugoslavia no longer exists,' he is alleged to have complained to Vukmanović-Tempo when they met for the last time.[3]

The ship of state was nevertheless put back on course by a policy symbolised in 1974 by a fourth constitution and by the Tenth Congress of the SKJ. The Congress, held in May, was the

---

[3] According to Professor Branko Petranović, in *NIN*, Belgrade, 6 May 1990.

apotheosis of Tito. The Constitution, enacted in February, marked a world record, with its ten-part 'basic principles' and its 406 articles, running to 100,000 words and 250 pages. It enshrined and consolidated the new concept of Yugoslavia as an eight-unit confederation. It thus appeared to alter the very basis of the Communists' restoration of the union, which had been conceived as a federation of equal nations, not as a coming together of pre-existing 'states'. Furthermore, after a change of constitution every ten years or so, to reflect the development of Communist Yugoslavia, the latest statute seemed to be made for ever, since in order to amend it the unanimous consent of all components was required in a most complicated process.

All this was done under the vigilant eye of a redisciplined SKJ and of a President whose power was once again formally absolute. The first of the thirteen articles that the Constitution devotes to the President of the Republic reads as follows, in the official translation of Marko Pavičić, Dr.Jur.:

In view of the historic role of Josip Broz Tito in the National Liberation War and the Socialist Revolution, in the creation and development of the Socialist Federal Republic of Yugoslavia, the development of Yugoslav socialist self-management society, the achievement of the brotherhood and unity of the nations and nationalities of Yugoslavia, the consolidation of the independence of the country and of its position in international relations and in the struggle for peace in the world, and in line with the expressed will of the working people and citizens, nations and nationalities, — the SFRY Assembly may, on the proposal of the Assemblies of the Republics and the Assemblies of the Autonomous Provinces, elect Josip Broz Tito President of the Republic for an unlimited term of office.[4]

---

[4] *The Constitution of the Socialist Federal Republic of Yugoslavia*. Belgrade: Secretariat of the Federal Assembly Information Service, 1974, article 333.

The old pharaoh

The last decade of Tito's reign had a surreal air to it. He had become victim as well as deity and high priest of the cult of his personality. These were 'his' years more than ever before, and yet his health gradually deteriorated, starting with a heart attack in the spring of 1973, suffering from sciatica, inflammation of the lungs and liver, and going through a bad patch of serious cardiac complications while attending the Fifth Non-Aligned Summit in Colombo in the summer of 1976.

Definitely proclaimed president 'for an unlimited term of office' in 1974 at the age of eighty-two, after seven successive terms, he was no longer always able to grasp the full implications of what he was doing, or what was being done in his name. He spent most of his time in solitary luxury, far from the capital, in his island, mountain or country retreats, resting between royal visitations and foreign tours, for he kept a gruelling schedule of these up to less than a year before his death.

Because of that, because of his insistence on keeping up appearances (the vanity of hair colouring and toupees, the big cigars, the hunting exploits that started television news bulletins, the appearances at New Year's Eve and other celebrations), the public at large for long did not realise to what extent his general condition had in fact declined, let alone to what extent he had come to rely on his 'helpers' and advisers and his wife Jovanka. Indeed, it was only revealed in 1989 that for the last eight years of his life, on doctors' advice and with his agreement, a small team of personalities had been set up to create some sort of a protective screen around him, to free him from more mundane functions, and allow him to concentrate on the most important affairs of state. That team increasingly came to decide what he could or could not be told, whom he should or should not see, to the point of pulling strings on his behalf, and most probably keeping him isolated.

Then, all of a sudden, in 1977, he separated from Jovanka. In fact, he left her-well cared for. Although they never formally divorced, he had, to all intents and purposes, 'repudiated' her.

They would not meet again until she came to see him as he lay dying. Their relationship had begun to deteriorate in 1974, and her fall from favour has not yet been entirely explained, in spite of subsequent memoirs, interviews and litigations. It was engineered by intrigue reminiscent of Stalin's court, by convincing Tito that she was plotting against him and/or spying on him. Most probably, she found it difficult to accept that her hero was being manipulated through flattery to promote particular interests, and wanted to protect him from his 'protectors', and in so doing clashed with influential people.[5]

Special laws were made for Tito, and yet he was above the law. People received court sentences for telling jokes about him. His nominal salary was insignificant, there was no budgeted 'civil list', but he was probably the most expensive head of state of his time. By 1974, the number of his official residences had grown to thirty-two, and more would be added, as, for health reasons, new complexes were built for him in the mountains of Bosnia, at 1,300 m. first (never to be used, for doctors decided it was too high), then lower down at 600 m., and also on the southern Adriatic. His 'Blue Train', his two Adriatic yachts and his two Danube yachts, his safari park, his hunting and fishing preserves, were on everyone's lips.

He had always played for the big stakes, first in the Communist movement, and then in the non-aligned movement, of which he was not only one of the founders and chief architects, but also one of the most visible and active spokesmen. It had grown and grown in membership throughout the 1960s, changed direction, and by the mid-1970s had to all intents and purposes collapsed, thus impairing Yugoslavia's much vaunted foreign policy.

Tito, however, persisted to the very last in wanting to lead a progressive movement of the non-aligned. His endless journeying

---

[5] As relations with his wife worsened, Tito appeared more of a family man. He received his sons more often, and an increasing number of relatives turned up at the birthday lunches. The Belgrade daily newspaper *Politika* of 13 March 1990 published a family photograph of 1977 with twenty-eight of them around Tito, over four generations, including his youngest sister Tereza, who would go on to survive all the brothers and sisters, and who was then living in an old people's home in Zagreb.

and summiting gratified his vanity and his taste for travel, but it no longer corresponded to any deep Yugoslav yearning òr even interest. Yet he went on pontificating on every imaginable subject, making moral judgments on all possible issues, giving advice to all foreign governments, but accepting only praise from the outside world. The arrogance of Yugoslavia's non-alignment was part of her leader's policy of grandeur that had already shrunk. Attributing any crisis to superpower rivalry, it sheltered behind a non-aligned movement which had become too radical for Tito's liking, and where Yugoslavia's influence was much diminished.

Yet this was the time when conditions in the Balkans were entering a phase of détente that offered Yugoslavia the opportunity for regional initiatives, less ambitious but more useful than her previous global diplomacy. Tito did travel to Greece and Turkey in 1976, offering to mediate between them, but he was also trying to exploit both countries' disenchantment with NATO for the purpose of creating more non-alignment in the Balkans.

Otherwise in Europe he generally encouraged Eurocommunism, which he saw as a potential Communist club without constraints, one which his SKJ could have advised, perhaps led, and one which in return would have backed his own resistance to Soviet pressure in international Communist gatherings. Yugoslav diplomacy invested much in the preparation of the Berlin Conference of European Communist Parties in June 1976, which Tito attended and where he wanted to be first. Non-alignment having by then in fact disintegrated, it is possible to read in the foreign policy of Tito's last years the ultimate ambition of mediating between Moscow and Peking, so as to revitalise international Communism, and perhaps put himself at its centre — which would have been in harmony with his policy at home.

Without compromising his country's independence in any way, he had, by then, in any event again entered into a close relationship with the Soviet leaders. They could understand him; he was a man they could live with. Bilateral relations between Yugoslavia and the Soviet Union were rarely at stake. On the occasion of his last pilgrimage to Moscow, in May 1979, he and Brezhnev had stated that occasional divergences did not hinder the dialogue between their two countries. Four years earlier, in the spring of 1975, Tito had actually gone much further when he had told a visiting Czechoslovak military delegation:

> Formally, we are not members of the Warsaw Pact, but if the cause of socialism, of Communism, of the working class, should be endangered, we know where we stand . . . We hold our aims in common with the Soviet Union.[6]

Yugoslavia's non-alignment had never been a plain refusal to align. It could even be said that it had been more of a hybrid alignment, yet it had in its time allowed the country to act as a link between the two blocs. In the late 1970s, however, the need for such a link no longer existed, and the régime could no longer afford its president's passion for big policy.

Tito, with his great personal prestige, did not renounce his grand design, even though some of his attitudes came more and more into conflict with the realities of the Yugoslav situation, and his world rôle hardly helped to solve his country's problems. His actions as a world leader, his preoccupations with uniting a bloc of the non-aligned, his denunciations of imperialism and neo-colonialism, all these were in contrast with Yugoslavia's more down-to-earth efforts to export meat and labour, to attract foreign capital, technology and tourists, to buy (and to sell) arms, and to balance its trade and payments.

He indulged in the megalomania of the ageing despot, basking in the ever-growing cult of his personality. His paternalism enabled him to discipline Party cadres without losing their support, and his popularity at large to take unpopular decisions. At the same time, Yugoslavia was living well beyond its means, foreign credits making up the difference, in an atmosphere of spreading corruption. Kardelj, the last of the lieutenants, who had

[6] Quoted in Stevan K. Pavlowitch, *The Improbable Survivor: Yugoslavia and its Problems, 1918–1988* (London: Hurst, and Columbus, Ohio: Ohio State University Press, 1988), p. 120.

managed to maintain his position to the end, died in 1979. The Tito era was drawing to a close.

Several months after Stalin's death, Tito is said by Djilas to have observed: 'It is incredible how quickly a man like that was forgotten.'[7] Thoughts of immortality strengthened his determination to set off his personal power against impersonal institutions. He had always attached great importance to institutions, and no longer wanted a successor, if he had ever wanted one. At times he acted as though he would go on for ever, at any rate as though he would live to be over a hundred, like the uncles he liked to talk about. With the Eleventh Congress of the SKJ in 1978, he worked at preparing his succession. He put into place a collective leadership which he saw as a transition to a leaderless mechanism of permanent musical chairs. This was intended both to prevent a struggle for the succession, and any one ever again wielding as much power as he had. He wanted to be unique. There would be no Tito II, and the memory of the one and only Tito would continue to inspire the great machinery he had set up.

Yugoslav diplomacy had tried hard, but failed, to get him the Nobel Peace Prize for his eighty-fifth birthday. Instead, he was given the degree of Doctor of Military Science, and the Federal Assembly made him a People's Hero for the third time. For months thereafter, his slightest gestures and words were eulogised as historical events. Tito still conjured up the enthusiasm of the Party faithful, and created some sort of a general feeling of pride at popular level, but also and increasingly the cynicism of many of the better educated, especially of the young.

He was, according to the point of view adopted, the charismatic leader who alone was able to conciliate the Yugoslav contradictions, or the dead weight that blocked the way to all solutions. The régime was eager to remind the population that what had been achieved had been achieved because of him, and that it could be repealed by him, or disappear with him. People, however, had come to want to turn these achievements from privileges into rights, and realised that Titoism had anyhow already run its course.

---

[7] *The Sunday Times* (London), 11 May 1980.

In these last years, discords were still harmonised to a large extent by the great man himself, the conductor of the Yugoslav orchestra, life president of the Republic and of its ruling Party, supreme commander, fellow of all the academies, doctor of all the sciences, and holder of all the honours. Yet at the same time, the country was also experiencing stagnation in government, and beginning to face the full onslaught of an economic and financial crisis.

Tito's death, like his reign, lasted a long time. He was taken ill on New Year's Eve 1979 with circulatory trouble in the right leg. He was subjected to a macabre series of unprecedented medical interventions, and lay dying for months, tended by a team of international specialists, surrounded by attendants, his ebbing life sustained by complicated machinery. From the moment the President went into hospital in Ljubljana until his death four months later, the government operated in an eerie atmosphere.

Even though it was obviously functioning for the first time without Tito as high arbiter, there was a constant coming and going of dignitaries between Belgrade and Ljubljana. It was necessary for the collective leadership to be seen to function normally without the supreme leader. At the same time, the supreme leader had to be seen to breathe his authority, his legitimacy, his charisma, his life almost, into his collective heirs. He had to be kept alive long enough to give the government time to make the necessary preparations, funereal, psychological, diplomatic, military; but then no one dared switch off the machines. In his death, he was more lonely than ever, even though the grey men he had placed in power hovered about, his two sons turned up, and his estranged wife was allowed to come and see him.

When he died on 4 May 1980, a few days before his eighty-eighth birthday, there was a long delay in announcing the President's death, which occurred just after 3 p.m. At 4.30 p.m. on that day, the usual daily medical bulletin announced that Tito's health had again reached a critical stage, whereas he had already been dead for almost an hour and a half. The proclamation announcing the death of the President of the Socialist Federal Republic of Yugoslavia, President of the League of Communists of Yugoslavia, Supreme Commander of the Armed Forces of Yugoslavia, Marshal of Yugoslavia, Comrade Josip Broz Tito, was not made until shortly before 6 p.m.

The unease felt by most Yugoslavs stemmed from fear that their way of life might be disturbed. Tito, for his compatriots, had become over the years the symbol of a Yugoslav style that had less to do with socialism, self-management and non-alignment than with freedom of movement, the advent of the consumer society through foreign credits and remittances, and fending for oneself. If the system in the last decade of his rule still appeared to solve the country's problems, it was by a mixture of magic, pretentiousness, consumerism, corruption, and foreign loans.

6

TITO AFTER TITO, 1981-1991

The myth continues

Soon after Tito had been taken ill, Yugoslavia's collective Presidency started to prepare his funeral, and settled for interment in the grounds of his Belgrade residence. He was known to have been impressed by Roosevelt's tomb at Hyde Park, with its white marble slab inscribed with only name and dates. The dead leader's body was then brought back from Ljubljana to Belgrade on his 'Blue Train', and buried in great pomp, in the presence of grieving crowds, and of representatives of 122 states. All three parts of the world — East, West and South — had come together to praise the great departed for one last time. As for the Yugoslavs, they were generally stunned. 'I could not believe that he could die,' said a Belgrade taxi-driver with tears in his eyes, echoing the feelings experienced by more than one Soviet citizen at the time of Stalin's death.[1]

Even though not quite to the extent of Brezhnev in his last years, Tito too had turned into 'a living dead leader', a prestigious figurehead in whose name power had been exercised by others still sensing his eyes, as he watched to ensure that his legacy was not betrayed.[2] Following on his death, there was an initial period when the political establishment pretended that the late president's spirit still led them. The collective leadership put into place by Tito had been dubbed 'Tito and the eight dwarfs'. The dwarfs were now without their life president, and they would take it in turns to chair their federal Presidency. In order to give themselves strength, they encouraged the continued growth of Tito's cult, inspired unwittingly by a pseudo-Christian conception of life

---

[1] Mihailo Marković, a retired leading Communist, recalled this a decade later in *NIN*, Belgrade, 6 May 1990.

[2] Roy Medvedev thus described the end of Brezhnev's rule in *The Times*, 8 September 1988.

87

after death, with distorted traces of real presence, incarnation and transfiguration.

The inscription on his tomb might have been inspired by Roosevelt's, and so was the name given to the whole complex of Tito's Belgrade residence — the Josip Broz Tito Memorial Centre; the daily military ceremonial, however, was more like that at Atatürk's mausoleum in Ankara. At Brioni too, the military went on mounting guard. The slogans — 'What will there be now? There will be Tito', and 'After Tito — Tito' — expressed what Tito had wanted and what his successors needed. The discourse about him continued as if he were still alive.

The Army laid wreaths on the tomb of 'our Supreme Commander'. The Central Committee entered him in the preamble of the SKJ Statutes. There was a proposal for an Order of Marshal Tito, and as late as 1989 a veterans' organisation nominated him for the posthumous award of a fourth title of People's Hero. Four towns were already named after him (usually with the prefix 'Tito's', a Yugoslav version of the English suffix 'Regis'), not to mention a mountain peak and a street in every town, along with a statue of him striding towards eternity. The trend was kept up for a number of years, until by 1983 'Tito's towns' numbered eight, one in every republic and region, and until proposals for new statues clashed with citizens' petitions to remove them — but that was not until the turn of the decade.

Every year for a decade, on 4 May at 3.05 p.m. sirens wailed and the country was supposed to observe a minute's silence. Over 14 million people religiously filed by his tomb in ten years. More of Tito's collective works rolled off the presses, and hundreds of books continued to appear on him, telling us more about the posthumous cult than about the historical character. Another special law was enacted in 1984 on the use of his name and likeness, laying down precise guidelines to preserve the dignity of his memory, and terms of imprisonment for flouting these, ranging from three months to three years.

Tito's death had coincided with the 'second oil shock' which precipitated the deterioration of Yugoslavia's economic crisis. The drying up of external resources exposed the incompetence and the inconsistency of the financial policies pursued, as the artificial improvement in living standards achieved during the 1970s evaporated, and as political regional interests combined to stall any effective reform. The country found itself again near the bottom of the European economic league table, as it had been before the revolution. It was also diplomatically isolated, as it became obvious that even the semblance of a non-aligned movement could no longer be maintained once Tito was no longer there to act as a resonance chamber, and once the cost of his sumptuous diplomacy could no longer be endured.

The political crisis was even more serious, as Party power had shifted after Tito's death to the regions as decisively as government power had in earlier years. The SKJ establishment had been granted territorial shares of sovereignty in recognition of services rendered. In the 1980s, these were no longer relevant, and the monarch who could impose a consensus over a divided Party was dead. The government he had left behind had run out of ideas. Although a substantial trend in the SKJ was in favour of some overhaul of the system, at the Twelfth Congress in 1982, the first since Tito's death, no one was brave enough to ask for structural changes, and unanimity hovered around the lowest common denominator — legitimising slogans such as the oft-repeated 'And after Tito — Tito!', or 'Our socialist, federal, self-managed, independent and non-aligned Yugoslavia's — Tito's Yugoslavia'. With such inept plastering-over of the structural cracks in the political leadership, it was not surprising that the generals were beginning to think that the Army might provide the only reliable guarantee of Tito's legacy.

The myth crumbles

Tito's face was still to be seen everywhere, public obeisance was still made at his tomb, and public criticism of him remained unacceptable, but it was already felt that the appeals to continue treading the late leader's path had now been overtaken by events. Tito was a historic personality, and he belonged to the past. The present was paralysed, and he bore much responsibility for it. Such was the climate in which Dedijer's bomb exploded in 1981. That was the controversial second volume of his 'New Contributions to a Biography of Josip Broz Tito', meant as a draft for a revised version of the 1953 biography.[3] He had been given access to all archives, including Tito's own papers, and help had been forthcoming from many important personalities. He wanted to uncover Tito the great man he admired, who had been hidden under Tito the monument. With his filial but obsessional attempt to reassess the father of the Revolution, Dedijer started a process of demystification. Myths began to shrink back to the dimensions of reality.

Disillusioned, the Yugoslavs were deserting the Party in droves, as more and more people distanced themselves from a system seen to be decayed, divided along ideological, ethnic and regional lines, and incapable of solving anything. Tito's successors were probably not sorry to shed some of their burden of responsibility back to yesterday's hero, but in so doing they were allowing their and his régime's essential claims to legitimacy to be questioned. They were authoritarian, narrow-minded and second-rate. They were so divided among themselves that they no longer understood what they were trying to do, beyond holding on to their power. Now that they could no longer put off facing the tensions and problems that assailed the system they were trying to preserve, it was understood that Tito's cult, while containing them, had also prevented the quest for solutions, and taboos were gradually lifted.

Thus 1984 turned out to be no Orwellian year for Yugoslavia, merely the year when the emperor was seen to be naked, and when the crisis was seen for what it was — a crisis of the system that had been symbolised by Tito. It was the year when 'Tito's way' can be said to have come to an end without anyone saying so in so many words. This was symbolised by the quarrel between his political and his private heirs over his property.

The question of the legal ownership of what had been put at

---

[3] In its original Serbo-Croatian version, *Tito Speaks* was entitled 'Josip Broz Tito: Contributions to a Biography'. Dedijer died in 1990, leaving unfinished his ever more disorganised 'New Contributions'.

Tito's disposal, or given to him, had not been important while he was alive, but his private heirs did raise it once he was dead. The Presidency thus set up a commission to inventory it all, and find out what could be considered Tito's. The task was completed after four years, in 1984. A list of what was considered inheritable property was produced. His widow, Jovanka, and his sons, Žarko and Aleksandar-Miša, were recognised as private heirs. A Law for the Administration of the Socially-Owned Assets Connected with Josip Broz Tito was hurriedly passed. The heirs contested the settlement, and the court case dragged on until 1990, when the sons accepted, but the widow rejected, a slightly improved settlement.[4]

The economy began to grind to a halt in 1985, with a foreign debt of $20–21 billion, spiralling inflation, and a continuous fall in real wages, until the veritable workers' revolt that occurred in 1987. This was accompanied by growing pressure from the intelligentsia. By that time, student publications already mocked the cult of Tito, and few people remained who still looked back with nostalgia to his era. His luxury sixteen-cabin seagoing yacht, put up for sale in 1984, had not yet found a buyer when, in 1987, the SKJ still managed to celebrate the fiftieth anniversary of his (officialised) coming to the head of the KPJ.

By the following year, the cult was under general assault. The publication of Tito's works was faltering. Heavily subsidised, it had produced just under half of the sixty or so planned volumes, when confusion and division set in among the team of editors and scholars. There were disagreements over what should or could be published, polemics over the backlog of unsold stocks, protests over the money thus spent, and resignations. Well-known intellectuals demanded a free, critical and scholarly approach to a reappraisal of Tito's historical rôle. Others called for 'de-Titoisation' as the essential first step to a multi-party democracy

---

[4] As a widow, Jovanka was shabbily treated. Although given a pension equivalent to the salary of the president of the Federal Assembly, she was deprived of her passport, she was submitted to petty chicaneries by the politicians and officials she had once come up against, the media were not allowed to voice her complaints, and she now found some sympathy in public opinion.

and the quest for an exit from the crisis.

The late president's 'social property' had been divided between the Federation, the republics and the Memorial Centre, but the cost of maintaining it all and the need for ready money led the authorities, from 1989 on, to try and sell the surplus of residences, for use as luxury hotels and clinics, preferably to foreign investors. Questions were asked, even in parliament, about the huge cost of the Memorial Centre. The myths had already shrunk back to reality. They would now go through reality, and inflate again in the form of negative myths. The Yugoslav public in 1989 and 1990 were relishing extraordinary and piquant stories about Tito's private life, his women, his illegitimate children, his shady art deals and his hidden treasures.[5] By the time of the tenth anniversary of his death, not only was he being depicted as greedy, vainglorious and mendacious, but all the ills of Yugoslavia and of its component ethnic communities were attributed to him, and he was no longer referred to as Tito. He was plain Josip Broz.

The crumbling of the Titoist myths has to be seen also in the context of the momentous changes that swept across the whole of the Communist-ruled part of the European continent on 1989 and 1990. As described by Keith Sword, these changes 'were the result of an irresistible pressure for reform and change on the part of people who had for too long endured the drabness, stifling restrictions, arbitrariness, untruths and economic shortages of Communist rule',[6] but Yugoslavia, which had been the first to experiment with reform and change, was now almost the last to go for real change. It experienced no revolution, merely a gradual disintegration of its Titoist régime. In the months leading to the tenth anniversary of Tito's death, thousands took to the streets

---

[5] Filip Radulović's 'The Loves of Josip Broz' (*Ljubavi Josipa Broza*, Belgrade: Grafos, 1990) went to a second edition. The author claims to have obtained Tito's agreement in 1977 to research all his women, and to have interviewed them (directly in most cases, with a few through close relations), with the obvious exception of the three officially acknowledged. He named all seventeen of them, and nineteen children. Radulović's catalogue reads rather like a reduced version of Leporello's.

[6] Introduction to *The Times Guide to Eastern Europe*, (London: Times Books), 1990, p. 7.

in Belgrade to shout insults the least of which seemed to be 'Tito-Ceauşescu', as Bucharest renamed its Boulevard Josip Broz Tito. On 4 May 1990, the day of the anniversary, *Politika*, Serbia's establishment daily, stated in its leading article: 'The myth of Tito is today to all intents and purposes totally dead.'

That was the year when all component republics of Yugoslavia (along with most other republics of eastern Europe) had their first multi-party elections, and when the disintegration of 'Tito's Yugoslavia' started the process of disintegration of Yugoslavia *tout court*. As the transitional period of 'Tito after Tito' under the dwarfs gave way to a new era of rival republican ethnarchs who exploited sectional nationalist frustrations, grievances and aspirations, and thrived on declining economies, the new leaders legitimised their movements and parties through elections that were as free and fair as could be expected in the circumstances, and set up republican régimes that were as one-party minded as could be expected from their Communist education. In such a climate, Tito became a general scapegoat. Only the Army still retained his icon, even though it no longer spoke of him.

The debunking of Tito was most thorough in Croatia, under the government of the anti-Communist Croatian Democratic Union of Franjo Tudjman, but most vehement in Serbia, under the government of the neo-Communist Socialist Party of Serbia of Slobodan Milošević. As the new parliament in Croatia repealed the special laws on Tito, removed his portraits from public places, and took over Brioni, the authorities of Tito's cities in Serbia reverted to the old names, and the Serbian government appointed a commission to tackle the problem of what to do with Tito's tomb and mausoleum. By the end of 1990, the 5,000 dinar 'Tito' note was withdrawn from circulation. On 28 August 1991, the statue of Tito was removed from the main square in Užice (one-time Titovo Užice) where the first Communist authority had been set up under him fifty years earlier.

Did the leaders and generals in Belgrade and in Zagreb blush when *Borba*, the one-time Party daily, now the most independent-minded paper in Yugoslavia, quoted the eulogies they had inscribed in the book of distinguished visitors at the mausoleum in (not so much) earlier years? 'If my father was still around, he would not have let this happen . . . My father would have dealt with this firmly,' Tito's younger son told *The Times*. His father's posthumous life had stopped short of the centenary of his birth.

7

TITO, TITOISM AND YUGOSLAVIA

Unification and reunification

Tito's fame rested on two claims. He appeared to have reunified Yugoslavia after the chaotic gap of the Second World War, and to have forged a new and relatively liberal form of Communism. This Titoist Communism was seen as a better unifier than the romantic intellectuals, the 'bourgeois' politicians and the monarchy who had originally cobbled the union in 1918, and Tito himself was seen as a pathfinder for the non-Stalinist Left. Now, however, that Communism has collapsed in Europe, leaving behind it ruins inhabited by fears and obsessions, Titoism is at best already forgotten, at worst brushed aside as having been as mendacious as the rest of Communism. The only people who appear to be nostalgic about it are superannuated Yugoslav generals, ageing PLO activists and elderly members of the British-Yugoslav Society.

Tito's Communist-ordered reunification would not have taken place without the original, epoch-making unification that came at the end of the First World War. The roots of the Yugoslav idea go back to the early years of the nineteenth century, but it was the Great War that brought about the co-ordination of two practical Yugoslav concepts, one emanating from Serbia, and the other from Croatia. The Serbian one was based on the fact that the unification of all Serbs could only come about once the Ottoman Empire and Austria-Hungary had been destroyed, and with the understanding that all South Slavs (in practical terms, Serbs, Croats and Slovenes) would come together into the same state. The Croatian one emerged with the realisation that Croats had to get together with other Slavs in Austria-Hungary — first and foremost with those Serbs who lived in their midst — to stand up to the dominant national groups, the Austro-Germans and the Magyars.

When unification came about as a result of the collapse of Austria-Hungary, it was both premature and overdue. It was premature, because what had been no more than a distant ideal in 1914 had been turned into a necessity in the space of a few months at the end of 1918. The leaders of the various sections of the Yugoslavs did not have the time to work out beforehand clear and agreed ideas about how the union would be implemented. It was also overdue because a nineteenth-century dream, championed by enlightened intellectuals, was realised, not at the time of the unification of Italy, but at the end of the First World War when the process of articulation of several identities among the South Slavs was already well advanced. Furthermore, it was carried out on the assumption that Serbs, Croats and Slovenes were one nation. The nation-state was part of the ideology of the time, and it had strong propaganda value. In the case of Yugoslavia, it may still have been an ideal. However, it was also already an illusion.

Yugoslavia did nevertheless bring them all together in a union that was free of foreign domination. That union opened up to related and entwined communities the possibility of developing economically and politically. Far from being a creation of the Versailles Conference, as is sometimes claimed, Yugoslavia had to impose itself on the international community. It had been proclaimed in December 1918, but the first of the major Allied powers to recognise it — the United States — did so in February 1919, and the last — Italy — in November 1920. Its borders were contested, and almost two years passed by before it felt accepted by the public law of Europe sufficiently to hold elections for a constituent assembly.

By the beginning of 1929, an impatient and authoritarian King Alexander had had enough of parliamentary government, and integration was thereafter imposed from above. Negotiations and compromises had not usually been at the forefront of the Yugoslavs' political culture, but when political parties did stand up for parliamentary government and individual rights, they found little difficulty in reaching compromise on ethnic issues and on a common Yugoslav state.

The KPJ as Tito found it was heterogeneous but, as the Comintern's anointed, he was accepted, and was able to reorganise it to the point where the end of the inter-war period found him leading a united party, committed body and soul to the Soviet Union and to Stalin. During the Second World War, the KPJ inserted itself into the spontaneous resistance of the Serbs of the Ustaša-ruled (or, to be precise, misruled) 'Independent State of Croatia', but at the same time it used the notion of 'Serbian hegemony' (which had been a Comintern slogan to break up Yugoslavia until 1935) to ingratiate itself with some other groups. This was already a policy which balanced out the nationalities — against each other to a certain extent.

In its quest for power during the People's Liberation Struggle, it adopted federal forms and the principle of ethnic pluralism, as Stalinist models meant to be lightning conductors for national emotions until Communism had eliminated them. Ideological integration and the principle of one-party rule was substituted for the monarchy's ethnic integration and its one-nation principle.

The KPJ also carried out a revolution in the name of an industrial working class that did not really exist, and with the help of a peasantry whom it then largely destroyed as a class. It turned its peasant partisan fighters into a power apparatus, and then sacrificed agriculture in favour of an industry that would have created a new Communist working class. Eventually the workers were cheated out of a sham self-management that was turned over to the Party and state apparatus — the only privileged part of society.

Tito at the head of the KPJ managed to harmonise these contradictions, because the KPJ-led People's Liberation Movement had brought the Yugoslavs out the war. It had provided a refuge and an organisation for the Serbs who were fighting against extermination by the Ustašas. It had also provided a way out of defeat alongside the Axis Powers for the Croats who had fought for, worked for, sympathised with, or simply accepted the Ustaša régime. It had asked no questions of collaborators who went over to the partisans. It had given an identity and a homeland to the hitherto unacknowledged Macedonian Slavs. It had rounded off the Slovenes' and the Croats' ethnic territory at the expense of defeated Italy. For all of them it restored Yugoslavia from the ruins of defeat, occupation, secession and partition. That was its first claim to legitimacy, in spite of all its compromises and manipulations, in spite of all the sufferings imposed in its struggle for power.

The events of 1948 were crucial, for they made 'Titoism', and strengthened its patriotic legitimacy. At the same time, they divided the KPJ and separated it from its source. They pitted Stalinist realists, who became Titoists, against Stalinist idealists, who became Cominformists. Those who put their faith in Tito and remained part of the power structure persecuted those who chose to remain faithful to their ideals, several thousands of whom lost their lives in the subsequent purges. With hindsight, one can date the beginnings of the decline of Yugoslav Communism to that crucial date, for those members of the KPJ who chose power and Titoism would later go on to accept nationalism, free elections, and even the removal of Tito's pictures and mortal remains, in order to retain power. Nevertheless, if Tito, with his Stalinist training and experience, had not then been at its head, the KPJ and the Yugoslav state would not have successfully stood up to Stalin.

A leader who wanted to lead

Like the English King Henry VIII, Tito did not intend or foresee the consequences of the break, and when he sought to strengthen his régime thereafter, he did so by going back to old ideas, not by anticipating new ones. Criticism of the Soviet Union did not start before 1950, and no sooner had Stalin died than it came to an end.[1] Tito did not see himself as the embodiment of defiance of the Soviet Union. He wanted to be acknowledged as one of the leaders of the Communist movement, because he considered

---

[1] 'From the point of view of Yugoslav interests, Stalin died too soon, only three years after Tito's real break with him,' writes Svetozar Stojanović in an interesting article entitled 'Stalin died too soon' (*Borba*, Belgrade, 11–12 May 1991).

that the success of the Yugoslav revolution entitled him to that status, and because he wanted to build himself into a world figure — a rôle for which his country alone did not provide a big enough stage. He certainly agreed with those who described him as a champion of socialism, and eventually as one of the titans of the world. Since the Communist world did not allow him to play that rôle, his government devoted enormous efforts to building up a progressive movement of Third World countries for him to lead.

Cycles of repression and liberalisation alternated until the late 1960s, bringing the average Yugoslav a relative freedom compared with the situation in the Soviet Union and in the satellites, and Tito was further legitimised in the eyes of much of the population, and of the anti-Soviet West. The peasants were allowed to pro-duce freely for the market. There was some economic growth, at the expense of profitability. Culturally the country did open up. The intelligentsia were free to think and create as long as they did not question the system, and even in periods of repression they did not suffer unduly, since repression was selective. The manipulation of more or less freedom went hand in hand with the demonisation of conspiring 'enemies' within and without.

Then, at the turn of the 1960s to the '70s, Tito and the power structure took fright at the conjuncture of domestic and foreign developments. Tito intervened personally to impose ideological purity and unity once again, appearing as the mainspring of the country and of the system. The endless constitutional experimen-tation came to an end as the system was frozen by the Constitution of 1974, to ensure the survival of Tito's achievements. In order to break up what he judged to be the incipient development of an all-Yugoslav opposition, he resorted again to purges and national manipulations.

Tito removed the best and the most reform-minded Com-munists from the top posts, and then his wife as well, until he was left quite alone, surrounded by first-class flatterers and third-class Party bureaucrats. With no vision any longer, he was unable to think along the lines called for by the new times. There was no natural heir left, and he did not want one. The élan provided by the partisan struggle, the revolution and the destruction of the old order had long since gone; even the pride of the anti-Stalinist stand and of non-aligned diplomacy had faded away; and with it all, so had Yugoslav patriotism.

Based on the illusion that it could continue Titoism without Tito, the 'dwarfs' system continued to function in a manner of speaking for exactly a decade after his death, as Titoism gradually collapsed. The régime by then was both authoritarian and paralysed, lumbered with an enormous bureaucracy at state, Party and economic level that had to be supported by an economy in crisis. It could not renounce its sources of legitimacy — the late President and the partisan struggle — nor did it dare look for new ones, such as ability to reform, effectiveness and popular support. It attributed its instability to subversion and conspiracy, whereas it was caused by divisions between the various sections of the establishment. Titoism, as a series of illusions performed by the ruling élite to retain power, could not survive its creator for more than a few years. For Tito's memory, it would certainly have been better if he had died before he had inaugurated the last repressive, and disintegrative, cycle of his reign — that of the 1970s.

How was he able to hold Yugoslavia together? Why did he ultimately fail to hold it together? Those two questions are now often heard, and they have the same answer. The reasons for Yugoslavia's disintegration are to be found in the way in which it was held together. Tito's Communist Yugoslavia was a revolutionary reconstruction on existing foundations. In spite of its origins, the new régime fell short on imagination, perhaps even more than the previous one, for it was essentially interested in power. It claimed to have solved the national question by removing the old order, but it prevented all integrative developments that fell outside its ideological control, such as those that market and culture could have produced, or democratic forces, or even the timid yet real flowering of Christian ecumenism in the 1960s.

Tied to the Cold War, it earned a good living from it, and thus provided relative and artificial freedom without investing for the future in political or economic foundations. The longer Tito's régime went on, the greater the contrast between its form and its content, between gloss and reality. The régime had frozen itself into a monument to its founder, while identifying Party and state with him and with his memory, thus making a transition to post-Titoism within its own frame an impossibility.

In the West Tito has been called a rebel, a pragmatist, an ideological innovator and a nationalist. He was none of those. In fact, he was a leader rather than a rebel, and his pragmatism was essentially tactical. He was a practical ruler, concerned with his place in History. He clung to some basic tenets of Marxist-Leninist dogma, usually in their Stalinist and Cominternist forms, which he adapted only so much as was necessary to keep power. He disdained theoretical disputations, and built his position in the KPJ against them. He was suspicious of new ideas, since they could undermine his position, but he was quick to see the 'public-relations' advantage of some of them, and knew how to make use of it.

He was no nationalist, Croat or Yugoslav. He came from the Zagorje region of Croatia, bordering on Slovenia, and was born of mixed parentage. The language he grew up with was far from the allegedly unvitiated dialect of Herzegovina that nineteenth-century philologists had moulded into an acceptable Serbo-Croatian literary language, a sort of South Slav Tuscan. What he spoke as a youngster was part local Croatian dialect, part Slovenian. His native milieu, furthermore, was not haunted by the ideal of South Slav unity which belonged to the urban intelligentsia; it was generally loyal to the Habsburgs, even though it resented Hungarian rule.

His travels then removed him even further from any connections with the struggles in his South Slav homeland. He had not been one of those young Yugoslav revolutionaries who had wanted to blow up the old Habsburg dynastic conglomerate in the name of the nationalistic South Slav ideal. By the time that he returned to his native land in 1920, he was a virtual foreigner. His formative years had been spent in Austria and in Russia. Serbian public opinion sees him, ten years after his death, as the agent of a Comintern conspiracy against the Serbian nation, strengthened by his Croatian origin. The latter is irrelevant, and there was no anti-Serbian Comintern conspiracy.

It was just that the Communist International under Stalin saw Yugoslavia at first as a foreign-policy risk for the Soviet Union, as part of the European *cordon sanitaire* drawn against it, until the rising threat of the Third Reich made it change its perception, and view a united Yugoslavia as part of a *cordon sanitaire* protecting it against that threat. The KPJ had no great difficulty in making such a U-turn, as it was naturally internationalist, and generally free of nationalist attitudes.

In Austria, Tito had been influenced by the concept of a multi-national state whose subjects owed loyalty to a polity that transcended their region, their linguistic group, or their ethnic community. A relative newcomer to Communism, he had learned in Russia that institutions mattered more than ideals in acquiring and keeping power, although ideology was important as a cement for these institutions. He took over a pan-Yugoslav Communist Party whose aim had become ascendancy over the whole state through revolution.

He needed a power-base and a sphere of action, and thus the Party and the state were important to him, and it was his association with the state that eventually made him identify with the life of the nation, as interpreted by him. Until 1948, he envisaged Communist Yugoslavia as part of a future world Communist order. Even after 1948, he never completely shook off that perception, as he later went back to ideological co-operation with the Soviet leadership, and in the non-aligned movement saw a substitute socialist internationalism. So it was the acquisition and the preservation of power that made him identify with Yugoslavia, and thus unintentionally and paradoxically begin the disintegration of Communist internationalism after 1948. Similarly, it was again the preservation of power that, twenty years later, led him to initiate a feudalisation of the SKJ, and thus the disintegration of Yugoslavia itself.

What was Titoism?

To acquire and then to preserve the monopoly of power had always been the first task of the KPJ and SKJ leadership. This was true of the take-over period, when Tito was anticipating and fomenting revolution outside Yugoslavia's borders, while fearing the unlikely victory of anti-Communist forces within them. It was true in the middle period, when he handled the nationalities issue according to divide-and-rule principles which came to accentuate the cleavages between component nations and regions. It was true in the final period, when he delegated power to his trustees in the republics who in turn went on to draw on nationalistic feelings and on international credit to build up their separate power-bases. Because of his charismatic arbitration, Tito gave the impression that the political system which he and his team had set up could be functional, whereas it turned out to be little more than a décor for his will.

Titoism, also known abroad at the time as 'the Yugoslav model', and later at home as 'Tito's way', was a myth, in the sense that it was a heroic rendering of historical events. It emanated from a deep reality, conceptualised and personalised. It was a set of ideas intended to substantiate pre-existing beliefs and to hide existential difficulties by reference to something which seemed new. It was the consequence, and not the cause, of the conflict with Stalin. It was the result of the efforts made by the Yugoslav Party leadership to stay in control. The central Party leadership never relinquished its monopoly of power, with Tito at the helm, steering the régime this way and that. It was he who was instrumental in first Stalinising and then de-Stalinising, in crushing Djilas and then Ranković, in pursuing Croatian 'nationalists' followed by Serbian 'liberals', in reluctantly approving self-management and then applying the brakes to its genuine implementation.

Tito survived by dignifying his efforts at staying in the saddle, in spite of Soviet efforts to dismount him, as his own superior brand of socialism, and by creating the illusion that new Marxist thoughts had been discovered. His régime had become independent of the Soviet Union, and it had implemented a different strategy of domestic development, but there were basic principles from which Tito never deviated, and limits beyond which he never went.

From the moment when he became leader of the KPJ, Tito thought of himself as a great man, and his lieutenants and assistants thought likewise. They worked as a closely-knit team, they accepted his authority and treated him as a man apart. The atmosphere between them was usually relaxed, but it was agreed by all, including himself, that his person and his rôle were exceptional. Why? His education was inadequate, his knowledge superficial, he read little, his Serbo-Croat was faulty, his style was all clichés, he was incapable of inventing anything, he was a bad public speaker, but he was always confident of his own judgement. For a long time, he had a good political instinct, and tolerated no opposition to the decisions that had been taken by the leadership since, in the final analysis, they had always been his. He was a man of action, a gifted politician, with an appetite for power and a weakness for show, mixing pride and vanity.

The two pillars of Titoism were self-management and non-alignment. Self-management socialism caused more problems than it solved, because it was never allowed to develop into what it should have been, namely control of the economy by the workforce, and because it was accepted by Tito only to the extent that it would not interfere with political power. It was designed to prove that Communist Yugoslavia under Tito was a socialist state. It was accepted as a useful means of exercising Party rule over society, economy and government. It provided some form of internal peace, but at a high economic cost. At one stage self-management as practised in Yugoslavia was almost seen as a model for the whole socialist world, but it could never have taken on anywhere else. It was too closely linked to domestic developments in Yugoslavia, apart from the fact that the general context of Titoist socialism still retained much in common with Soviet socialism. Its economic failure was eventually obvious when it brought Yugoslavia into an acute crisis, not only of its economy, but of its whole structure. It had come to undermine the belief in the advantages of living together in one single state, thus defeating the main historical advance made in the course of the last century by the South Slavs.

Tito, however, wanted to be judged by his achievements as a world leader. The Party and Yugoslavia were his concrete daily realities, but he always wanted to go beyond them. He retained a nostalgia for a socialist world, and passed on to the Third World not so much any renovated concept of Marxist socialism as the Leninist concept of the one-party state. He cleverly used the West to protect him against the Kremlin, and jockeyed for a leading position on the Communist front, attempting always to have the best of two, if not of three, worlds. But in the world rôles that he played or wanted to play, all that he had to work with was the concrete reality of Yugoslavia, his initial catapult but also his limiting factor. Tito's world policy was totally out of proportion with his country's strength — political, economic, military or cultural — even though it brought the country prestige for a time.

He had reigned for so long that he had picked up all the accumulated myths of the history of the South Slavs. He certainly understood their importance in politics, and fostered many, but none so well as his own. The cult of Tito's personality equalled that of the most prominent dictators of the twentieth century. It was one of the elements used by the Yugoslav leadership to maintain its continuity, and to profit from Tito's prestige in the East where he was known and esteemed, in the West where he was less known and more admired, and in the Third World to which he had extended help and a certain significance in world affairs.

Mediterranean boastfulness with esoteric verbiage can at times work wonders in the West, as Mussolini discovered long before Tito. This is something now generally forgotten, just as it must be a mystery to many younger readers why Tito came to be seen as a prophet. Most hues of the Western political spectrum had come to find something useful in Titoism at one time or another, and Britain was in the forefront of fostering the Tito cult.

There was no real continuity between British support of Tito in the years 1943–4 and that given to him after 1948, but the break with Stalin did come as an unexpected gift of history, to present a coherent story of a thriving and continuous friendship between Britain and Communist Yugoslavia. The self-publicity of British friends of Tito's Yugoslavia contributed to this in no little way, with the war tales of participants who naturally lined up their memories with what had happened since. Even as they began to retire, official diplomacy, with its tendency to equate a nation with its current government, helped to sustain these ideas beyond their natural life. This prevailed until the collapse of Communism throughout eastern Europe brought about, not any revolution against Titoism in Yugoslavia, but the terminal decline of that régime into feuding nationalist power structures, all of which had inherited something of it.

As the price for Yugoslavia's independence from the Soviet bloc since the 1950s, the West had armed Tito's régime, bailed it out, and gone on to underwrite the mismanagement of its economy. In the 1970s, banks had been only too happy to provide it with loans, in order to help recycle the surpluses of oil-producing countries. Titoism had thus been propped up for some forty years, and Yugoslavia had become accustomed to the ready availability of international finance. All this support had enabled it to 'muddle through' and to postpone the need for real reform.

The West had failed to see that Tito and his Communist Party had not created lasting political institutions through which different interest groups might resolve their conflicts, or a climate of tolerance able to contain ethnic differences. Tito's Western admirers had been unable to see through the illusions, beyond the economic 'muddling through' and the superficial political stability. Western policy had, in the end, simply encouraged a sclerotic *status quo*, without fully taking into account the need to maximise prospects for a positive change.

From Stalinism to nationalism

When the KPJ under Tito took over in 1945, Yugoslavia was an internationally recognised member of the Allied coalition, a founder-member of the United Nations that had just been linked by treaty to the Soviet Union, one of the victorious Great Powers. The Yugloslav Communists' international position was thus better than that of their predecessors in 1918. They had made a completely new start after the bloodbath of the Second World War and the defeat of sectional nationalisms. As revolutionaries, they could have provided the imagination that the founding fathers of the first Yugoslav state had lacked.

Their acknowledgement of ethnic pluralism and their adoption of federalism could have been expressions of that imagination, had they not been little more than transplantations of Soviet models. The Communists had given up the idea of a break-up of Yugoslavia, and for international purposes had even accepted the legal continuity of the state, but stuck to the view that the original unification had been a creation of Versailles placed under Serbian hegemony. They had accepted the principle of self-determination, but took it that the self-determination of Yugoslavia's constituent nations had been expressed once and for all through the People's Liberation Struggle.

While its adoption of ethnic pluralism and federalism did much for the consolidation of a union which it had taken over from the previous régime, the Communist régime went on to consider this pluralism as a substitute for political pluralism, and as an excuse for the maintenance of the Party's monopoly of power. Its stance in 1948 and the subsequent surge into modernity were further contributions to strengthening the bonds. But Yugoslavia entered the modern world by brutally destroying the old order and its traditional values, and by fanatically aping the Soviet Union for a few years. It then followed the zigzags of the economic consequences of Titoism, under severe control from above aimed at preventing any realignment of political priorities.

Yugoslavia did progress under Tito, often frenetically, but she did not do so as quickly as other countries of southern Europe that had not had a Communist revolution. Eventually, by the end of his rule, she found herself competing in truly non-aligned fashion with Portugal and Romania for the title of poorest country in Europe but one, the exception being Albania.

A vacuum had been created in which most people thought only

of promoting their own personal interests, either by joining the privileged class or by cheating the system. That is what Titoism had generally come to mean for them. The frustrations and resentments that built up over the last two decades were then gradually deflected by nationalistic rhetoric from considerations of real problems, channelling attention away from the inadequacies of social and economic infrastructures and the restrictions on liberty.

For the South Slavs to have gone on living together in a united state, they should have been allowed to participate fully in all spheres of their country's development, to express their diversity and their different approaches to their state, in other ways than by hurling themselves into their sectional nationalist impasses. In their anxiety to preserve their rule, the oligarchies of the several federated units sought an ultimate refuge in nationalism, and that encouragement coming from above started the breaking-up of Yugoslavia.

Communism, in Yugoslavia as in all the other lands of eastern Europe, had failed to create free individuals capable of critical thought about themselves and their national communities. Indeed, it had created the very opposite — subjects without ideas who were quick to embrace uncritically the nationalisms that had been preserved in their most primitive form beneath the monolithic structure of Communism. The leaderships chosen by Tito in 1971 hardly felt any need to justify their legitimacy by appealing to any ideas. Even less would they feel that need after Tito's death. Titoism for them had been but a long transition from Stalinism to nationalism. In Tito's time they had lied for the greater glory of a Yugoslavia that had some prestige, however illusory, and much real support. After Tito, they placed their mendacity in the service of their respective republic-based would-be nation-states.

The collapse of the system has led to the resurgence of chauvinism. The elections held in 1990 in all the republics (but not at the general, federal level) were the first free and multi-party elections since the Second World War. Indeed, they were the first really free elections since 1927. The régimes that emerged from the ballot boxes were all primarily nationalistic, and the new governments have since done their best to restrict the opposition, to limit the freedom of the media, and to preserve state control over the economy. They glorified the history of their respective groups, and found no difficulty in switching from an imposed, artificial, ideological unity, to a propaganda war between small, 'wretched'[2] nations, whose differences were no less artificially magnified, even before they went on to real war. Their megalomania, inherited from Titoism, was inevitably accompanied by delusions about omnipresent enemies and worldwide conspiracies.

Tito represented a system in which privileges had come to be all-important. His legacy included the manipulation of emotions, the militarisation of society, the political control of social organisations, the demonisation of enemies real or imaginary. Ten years after his death, he was turned into a scapegoat, as his ghost began to haunt and destroy the country that he had taken over and refashioned.

---

[2] A term used by the Hungarian political thinker István Bibó (died 1979). See the French edition of his essay, *La Misère des nations centre-européennes*, Paris: L'Harmattan, 1985.

BIBLIOGRAPHICAL NOTE

According to the Yugoslav Bibliographical Institute, more than 900 books on Tito had been published in Yugoslavia by 1989. More to the point for my English-speaking readers, April P. Carter lists 354 titles of books and articles in English in her *Marshal Tito: A Bibliography* (Meckler, 1989). Here, for a very limited list of books for further reading, I have selected only works available in English: unless otherwise stated, they are published in London.

Of Tito's own, *Selected Works on the People's War of Liberation* were printed in Yugoslavia but published in Bombay (Somaiya Publications, 1969), and *The Essential Tito* (ed. by Henry M. Christman) came out in England (Newton Abbot: David & Charles, 1970).

There is much in English that can serve as source material, starting with Michael Padev, *Marshal Tito* (London: Frederick Muller, 1944), who draws his material from London-published pro-partisan pamphlets. Stephen Clissold, *Whirlwind: An Account of Marshal Tito's Rise to Power* (Cresset Press, 1949), completed in October 1947, is impressionistic but intelligent. The author was directly involved in Yugoslav developments from 1938 to 1946, and draws on a variety of Communist sources, as well as on his own experiences. Other British general wartime eye-witness accounts of Tito's 'rise to power' are too romantic and uncritical to be listed here. While they are of great use to the scholar, they are of no help to most readers.

The 'schism' of 1948 gave rise to not a few polemical interpretations. Mosha Piyade (Moša Pijade), *About the Legend that the Yugoslav Uprising Owed its Existence to Soviet Assistance* (London, 1950), was written by a member of the Yugoslav leadership and published under the Yugoslav Embassy imprint. James Klugmann, *From Trotsky to Tito* (Lawrence & Wishart, 1951), is the work of a British Stalinist Communist who worked for the Special Operations Executive Yugoslav branch in Cairo during the war. Franz Borkenau, *European Communism* (Faber & Faber, 1953), completed in August 1951, has two chapters on Tito's rise to power. The author, a one-time German Communist who worked for the Comintern, writes with insight and scholarship, even if he makes no claims to formal scholarship.

Vladimir Dedijer, *Tito Speaks: His Self Portrait and Struggle with Stalin* (Weidenfeld & Nicolson, 1953, from the Yugoslav original of 1952) is now a classic; less so the sequel, *The Battle Stalin Lost: Memoirs of*

111

Yugoslavia, 1948–1953 (New York: Viking Press, 1971, from the Yugoslav original of 1969). Fitzroy Maclean, *Josip Broz Tito — A Pictorial Biography* (Macmillan, 1980), is a nicely produced photograph album.

The Royal Institute of International Affairs has produced two documentary surveys: *The Soviet-Yugoslav Dispute: Text of the Unpublished Correspondence* (1948), followed by *Yugoslavia and the Soviet Union, 1939–1973: A Documentary Survey* (edited by Stephen Clissold, 1975).

Milovan Djilas's testimony is all-important, and generally available in English translations: *Conversations with Stalin* (Rupert Hart-Davis, 1962), *The Unperfect Society: Beyond the New Class* (Methuen, 1969), *Memoir of a Revolutionary* (New York: Harcourt Brace Jovanovich, 1973), *Tito: The Story from Inside* (Weidenfeld & Nicolson, 1981), *Rise and Fall* (Macmillan, 1985), along with Stephen Clissold, *Djilas: The Progress of a Revolutionary* (Maurice Temple Smith, 1983).

Phyllis Auty, *Tito: A Biography* (Longman, 1970), based mainly on earlier accounts by Dedijer and British admirers, is worth re-reading, even if it verges at times unashamedly on the idyllic. Nora Beloff, *Tito's Flawed Legacy: Yugoslavia and the West, 1939–1984* (Victor Gollancz, 1985), vigorously critical, and written 15 years later, is a good antidote.

Many Yugoslav personalities of Tito's era have now written their memoirs, generally too long and untranslatable. In English, we do, however, have Edvard Kardelj, *Reminiscences* (Summerfield Press, 1982, from the Yugoslav original of 1980, covering the period to 1957), and Veljko Mićunović (who passed from the state security to the foreign service, and became ambassador to Moscow and to Washington), *Moscow Diary* (Chatto & Windus, 1980, from the Yugoslav original of 1977). One should not forget *Khrushchev Remembers* (André Deutsch, 1971).

The following selection of analytical works will be useful:

Ivan Avakumović, *History of the Communist Party of Yugoslavia* (vol. I, to 1941, Aberdeen University Press, 1964; there never was a sequel). Aleksa Djilas, *The Contested Country: Yugoslav Unity and Communist Revolution, 1919–1953* (Cambridge, Mass.: Harvard University Press, 1991). Tony Judt (ed.), *Resistance and Revolution in Mediterranean Europe, 1939–1948* (Routledge, 1989; in particular, Mark Wheeler's contribution). Adam B. Ulam, *Titoism and the Cominform* (Cambridge, Mass.: Harvard University Press, 1952). Wayne S. Vucinich (ed.), *At the Brink of War and Peace: The Tito-Stalin Split in a Historical Perspective* (New York: Columbia University Press, 1982). Ivo Banac, *With Stalin against Tito: Cominformist Splits in Yugoslav Communism* (Ithaca, NY: Cornell

University Press, 1988). Beatrice Heuser, *Western Containment Policies in the Cold War: The Yugoslav Case, 1948–1953* (Routledge, 1989). Dennison Rusinow (ed.), *Yugoslavia: A Fractured Federalism* (Washington: Wilson Center Press, 1988).

I trust I am not mistaken in thinking that my now twenty-year-old *Yugoslavia* (Ernest Benn, 1971) and *The Improbable Survivor: Yugoslavia and its Problems, 1918–1988* (C. Hurst, 1988) do, however improbably, still provide a serviceable guide to the history of Yugoslavia.

INDEX

Adriatic Sea, 40, 41
Africa, 39, 62, 64, 70, 72
Albania, 30, 31, 42, 53, 55, 107;
  Albanians in Yugoslavia, 53, 73
Alexander, King, 19, 20, 50, 96
Algiers, 44
America, United States of, 4, 10, 13,
  60, 70, 71, 96
Anti-Fascist Council for the National
  Liberation of Yugoslavia, *see*
  AVNOJ
Asia, 62–4, 70–1
Atatürk, President, 88
Austria, 1–3, 5, 13, 52, 95, 101–2
Austria-Hungary, *see* Habsburg
  Monarchy
Auty, Phyllis, 9, 35, 66, 75
Avakumović, Ivan, 28
AVNOJ, 38–9, 43–4, 50
Axis, 30, 37–40, 48, 97

Balkan federation, 53, 55
Balkan Pact, 61–2
Banac, Ivan, 58
Bari, 45, 47
Belgrade: 6, 18, 30, 32, 48, 59, 64, 73;
  Conference of Non-Aligned, 64;
  Declaration, 63; University, 28, 73
Belousova, Pelagija, *see* Broz
Berlin: Conference of European Com-
  munist Parties, 82; Congress, 1
Bevin, Ernest, 60
Bibó, István, 109
Bihać, 38, 43
Bohemia, 9
Benz, 10
Borba, 93
Bosnia, 34–41, 43–4, 48, 81
Bosnia and Herzegovina, 1, 2, 15, 30,
  50

Brdo, 65
Brezhnev, Leonid, 68, 71, 82, 87
Brioni, 65, 75, 93
Britain, *see* Great Britain
British-Yugoslav Society, 95
Broz family, 2–4, 7, 52, 81, 84, 91
Broz, Franjo, 2–5, 9, 16
Broz, Josip, *see* Tito
Broz, Jovanka, 52, 66, 75–6, 80–1,
  85, 91, 99
Broz, Marija, 1, 4, 16
Broz, Martin, 1, 10, 52
Broz, Pelagija, 14, 16, 20–1
Broz, Tereza, 81
Broz, Žarko, 16, 21, 33, 45, 52, 75,
  85, 91
Bucharest, 56–7
Budisavljević, Jovanka, *see* Broz
Bulganin, Marshal, 63
Bulgaria, 30, 42, 47–8, 53, 55

Cambridge University, 28
Carpathians, 11–2
Ceauşescu, President, 71, 93
chetniks, 31–4, 37–8, 40–2
Churchill, Winston, 41, 44–7
Colombo Conference of Non-
  Aligned, 80
Cominform and Cominformists, 53,
  56, 58, 63, 98
Comintern, 15, 17–30, 35, 38, 40–2,
  53, 97, 101–2
Communism, 28, 32–3, 36, 38–9, 41,
  45–6, 49, 50, 53–5, 60–2, 65, 68–9,
  76, 82, 95, 97–8, 102, 106, 108
Communist Party of Yugoslavia, *see*
  KPJ and SKJ
Constitution of 1921, 15, 19; of 1931,
  20; of 1946, 50; of 1953, 62; of
  1963, 67–8, of 1974, 78–9, 99